AARON SAHR is a philosopher turned economic sociologist. He is Visiting Professor at Leuphana University Lüneburg, Germany, and head of the Monetary Sovereignty research group at the Hamburg Institute for Social Research. His research interests include the sociology of money, facts and fictions about monetary policy, the history of capitalism, inequality, and social ontology.

Keystroke Capitalism

How Banks Create Money for the Few

Aaron Sahr

Translated by Sharon Howe

VERSO

London • New York

The translation of this work was funded by
Geisteswissenschaften International – Translation Funding
for Work in the Humanities and Social Sciences from
Germany, a joint initiative of the Fritz Thyssen Foundation,
the German Federal Foreign Office, the collecting society VG
WORT and the Börsenverein des Deutschen Buchhandels
(German Publishers & Booksellers Association).

First published by Verso 2022
First published in German as *Keystroke Kapitalismus:
Ungleichheit auf Knopfdruck* © Hamburger Edition 2017
© Aaron Sahr 2022
Translation © Sharon Howe 2022

All rights reserved

The moral rights of the author have been asserted

1 3 5 7 9 10 8 6 4 2

Verso
UK: 6 Meard Street, London W1F 0EG
US: 20 Jay Street, Suite 1010, Brooklyn, NY 11201
versobooks.com
Verso is the imprint of New Left Books

ISBN-13: 978-1-83976-119-5
ISBN-13: 978-1-83976-121-8 (US EBK)
ISBN-13: 978-1-83976-120-1 (UK EBK)

British Library Cataloguing in Publication Data
A catalogue record for this book is
available from the British Library

Library of Congress Cataloging-in-Publication Data
A catalog record for this book is available
from the Library of Congress

Typeset in Sabon by Biblichor Ltd, Edinburgh
Printed and bound by CPI Group (UK) Ltd, Croydon, CR0 4YY

Alles gehört dir
Eine Welt aus Papier
Alles explodiert
[Everything belongs to you
A world made of paper
Everything's exploding]

    Tocotronic (German indie rock band)

Contents

Introduction — 1

I. Debt — 11
  Capital Supply — 14
  The Debt Mentality — 17
  From Control to Protection — 19
  Sociotechnical Innovations — 25
  Appreciation and Depreciation Mechanisms — 29
  #ownership — 35

II. Ownership — 37
  From System to Practice — 39
  Economic Practices — 42
  Capitalist Practices — 47
  #capacity — 51

III. Capacity — 53
  Written Values — 55
  Distributive Institutions — 60
  Capital Producers — 64
  #appropriation — 67

IV. Appropriation — 71
  The Dualism Within the Political Economy — 74
  Asset Inflation – the Para-Economic Complex (I) — 79
  Looting Circles – the Para-Economic Complex (II) — 84

Interest Income – the Para-Economic Complex (III)	90
#*change*	95
V. Change	99
Legitimatory Homelessness	102
Unstable and Dysfunctional	109
Should Banks Be Economized?	113
Should Money Creation Be Democratized?	118
#*keystrokes*	124

Introduction

The total volume of privately owned wealth in the world today is approximately 418 trillion US dollars. That is almost five times global economic output.[1] In prosperous countries such as the US, the UK or France, private wealth amounts to roughly five or six times annual GDP. Even in post-communist China, it has now risen to four and a half times the country's economic product.[2]

This record wealth stands in relation to two other phenomena which together point to a social crisis and, as such, form the subject of this book. Alongside booming private wealth, the world is struggling with an unprecedented level of debt: Governments, companies and consumers were indebted to the tune of almost 200 trillion dollars in 2019.[3] That the world can accumulate such a vast private fortune while being *simultaneously* this deep in debt – unthinkable in the mid-twentieth century – is, needless to say, no accident. One person's debts are, of course, another person's assets. A good half of private wealth consists of financial assets in the shape of bank deposits, investment fund or insurance claims, government loans, shares and so on[4] – in other words, assets whose value rests on someone

---

[1] Anthony Shorrocks, James Davies and Rodrigo Lluberas, Credit Suisse Global Wealth Report 2021, Zurich 2021.

[2] Facundo Alvaredo, Lucas Chancel, Thomas Piketty, et al., 'Global Inequality Dynamics: New Findings From WID.world', *NBER Working Paper* 23119, 2017.

[3] See the International Monetary Fund's Global Debt Database, available at IMF.org.

[4] See Credit Suisse, *Global Wealth Databook 2016*.

else's promise to pay up. And their volume is constantly mounting. Many experts have been warning for years that private and public debt has reached such a peak that it can never be paid off with income from normal economic processes.[5]

Furthermore, there is a dynamic causal relationship between the growth of private wealth and the increasing indebtedness of OECD countries, which, in turn, points to a third phenomenon: the crisis of inequality. Income and wealth as well as debt itself are becoming increasingly unevenly distributed. In world terms, the income of the so-called global middle classes has risen in recent years, and, to that extent, there has been a slight relative reduction of the disparity between nations.[6] However, a look inside some of the wealthier countries reveals a very different picture. In the immediate aftermath of World War II, the share of wealth concentrated among the highest-earning, richest percentage of the wealth pyramid fell in many developed OECD countries. Yet hopes that this would lead to continuous and lasting progress towards more egalitarianism were disappointed.[7] Since the late 1970s, the distribution

---

5 Wolfgang Streeck, *Buying Time*, trans. Patrick Camiller and David Fernbach, London, 2017; Colin Crouch, 'Privatised Keynesianism: An Unacknowledged Policy Regime', *The British Journal of Politics and International Relations* 11(3), 2009, 382–99; Steve Keen, *Debunking Economics: The Naked Emperor Dethroned*, London, 2011; Ann Pettifor, *The Production of Money: How to Break the Powers of Bankers*, London, 2017; Susan Lund, Toos Daruvala, Richard Dobbs, et al., 'Financial Globalization: Retreat or Reset?', McKinsey Global Institute, 1 March 2013, available at mckinsey.com.

6 Branko Milanovic, *Global Inequality: A New Approach for the Age of Globalization*, Cambridge, MA/London, 2016.

7 This expectation of progress arose, not least, from the relevant studies by Simon Kuznets (see, for example, 'Economic Growth and Income Inequality', *The American Economic Review* 45(1), 1955, 1–28). More recent research on inequality makes many references to this disappointed hope: Thomas Piketty, *Capital in the Twenty-First Century*, trans. Arthur Goldhammer, Cambridge, MA, 2014, 11ff.; Anthony B. Atkinson, *Inequality: What Can Be Done?*, Cambridge, MA, 2015, 65ff.; Milanovic, *Global Inequality*, 46ff.; François Bourguignon, *The Globalization of Inequality*, trans. Thomas Scott-Railton, Princeton, 2015. James K. Galbraith, *Inequality:*

of income, and particularly of private wealth, has once again become increasingly asymmetrical. Between 1978 and 2015, for example, the poorer half of the US population saw the real (inflation-adjusted) purchasing power of its income fall by 1 percent. Over the same period, the real income of the richest 1 percent rose by nearly 200 percent.[8] In France, a country that arguably is representative of the Western European model,[9] income has grown by around 1 percent per year since the mid-1970s. If we subtract the 1 percent of the population with the highest income, however, that leaves just 0.6 percent of income growth for the remaining 99 percent. And the situation is comparable in most countries in the OECD.[10]

The same pattern is observable for wealth distribution: in the early 1960s, for example, the richest 10 percent of the UK's population owned approximately 67 percent of private wealth, while the richest 10 percent in France and the US owned around 70 percent. Twenty years later, this share dropped for a time to below 50 percent in the UK, around 50 percent in France, and a good 60 percent in the US.[11] Then came the turnaround, and, by about 2010, the UK's richest citizens had regained almost 54 percent of total private wealth, with France at roughly 56 percent and the US at just under 74 percent – a trend that continues to this day.[12]

What Everyone Needs to Know®, New York, 2016, 29f. To quote Piketty, people believed that 'the balancing forces of growth, competition and technological progress [would] lead in later stages of [economic] development to reduced inequality and greater harmony among the classes' (*Capital in the Twenty-First Century*, 13).

  8 Alvaredo et al., 'Global Inequality Dynamics'.
  9 Ibid., 4.
  10 OECD, *Divided We Stand: Why Inequality Keeps Rising*, Paris, 2011.
  11 World Inequality Database, available at WID.world; OECD.Stat, available at stats.oecd.org.
  12 Michael Förster, Ana Llena-Nozal and Vahé Nafilyan, 'Trends in Top Incomes and Their Taxation in OECD Countries', *OECD Social, Employment and Migration Working Papers* 159, 2014; OECD, *In It Together: Why Less Inequality Benefits All*, Paris, 2015.

INTRODUCTION

Given this state of affairs, modern sociologists cannot, as Pierre Rosanvallon observes, treat economic inequality as a 'legacy of the past' amid a long-term global trend toward equality.[13] On the contrary, we are currently witnessing 'a spectacular break with the past, reversing the trend of the past century'.[14] And it is the job of social science to establish the causes of that break.

Observers whose social instincts veer towards economic liberalism sometimes criticize research on inequality for disregarding the interests of real people. According to them, instead of getting worked up over the fact that almost all the world's capital is concentrated in the hands of a few people and thereby stoking envy-fuelled debate, we should focus our critique on poverty, not inequality.[15] On this front, they argue, a little can go a long way. Even small investments can have a far greater impact than costly, complex and normatively controversial redistributive policies, for instance. While there is certainly some truth to this, the suggestion that poverty is the 'real' evil points to a problematic theoretical construct of (neo) liberalism: the idea that economics is essentially a function of *individuals* – and not, as economic sociology would have it, a matter of *structures*. Liberal economic theorists from Adam Smith to Milton Friedman regard economics as a function of autonomous households using capital to improve their financial situation. According to this tradition, combating poverty means improving the 'market potential' of households without capital through transfer payments and education aimed at enhancing people's 'marketability'. As such, the call to focus on poverty rather than inequality, which – not by chance – came into vogue with the dawn of the neoliberal age, assumes

---

13 Pierre Rosanvallon, *The Society of Equals*, trans. Arthur Goldhammer, Cambridge, MA, 2013.
14 Ibid., 4.
15 For a discussion of this point of view, see Atkinson, *Inequality*, 23ff.

a classically liberal (political) economy that simply ignores structural factors such as asymmetrical capital ownership or the unequal distribution of advantages arising from economic systems or social circumstances.[16] This is not in any way to deny the often life-threatening urgency of poverty as a social problem. The fight against poverty saves lives and needs to be escalated. But to expect the social sciences to stop worrying about economic inequality for that reason is not a scientific demand but a political one that plays into the hands of those who benefit disproportionately from the system. Indeed, attempts to divert attention from inequality by talking about poverty actually hinder effective anti-poverty measures, as highlighted not least by the World Bank.[17] The way forward, therefore – and the intended purpose of this book – is to identify the *structures* that favour the few and disadvantage the many. One of these structures is the financial system.

Financial wealth is even more unevenly distributed than wealth as a whole. In the US, over 90 percent of company shares, bonds and receivables from investment funds and trusts belong to the richest 10 percent, as do a good 60 percent of life insurance policies, bank deposits and pension claims. In short, a relatively small minority owns a substantial majority of financial assets – and it is more or less the same story the world over.[18] The higher up the wealth distribution pyramid you go, the higher the ratio of financial to material assets. This is all the more significant because the holder of a financial asset – the creditor – is entitled to interest and principal payments from the borrower. In other words, unlike material

---

16 Ibid., 25.
17 World Bank, *Poverty and Shared Prosperity 2016: Taking on Inequality*, Washington, DC, 2016.
18 Kathrin Brandmeir, Michaela Grimm and Arne Holzhausen, *Allianz Global Wealth Report 2015*, Munich, 2015, 19. See Anthony Shorrocks, James Davies and Rodrigo Lluberas, Credit Suisse Global Wealth Report 2021, Zurich 2021 for recent figures.

goods such as houses, cars, machinery, land and so on, all financial assets are also transfer relationships. Income from these relationships grows in size and proportion to total income the closer you get to the top of the pyramid.[19]

The majority of borrowers in these transfer relationships are at the poorer end of wealth distributions. While citizens of the eurozone, for example, including the richest 10 percent, hold an average debt of 20 percent of their assets, the lowest-earning 20 percent owe roughly 110 percent of their assets, and are thus on average hopelessly *over*indebted.[20] In the early 1980s, the lowest-earning 95 percent of the US population recorded lower average levels of debt than the top 5 percent. By the mid-2000s, however, the 95 percent had doubled their debt ratio and were significantly overindebted, while the highest-earning 5 percent had actually reduced their debt levels.[21] It is a fact that the financial system has become increasingly asymmetrical over the past twenty-five years. Because financial assets (mostly concentrated among the few) and debts (mostly among the many) are two sides of a relationship shaped around the promise of payment, the system of financial investment has intrinsic wealth effects: the prosperous tip of the wealth pyramid and the poorer lower half are not unrelated, with the 'haves' on one side of the fence and the 'have-nots' on the other; rather, the minority at the top, by holding the bulk of financial wealth, are the creditors of the majority. As promises of payment, financial assets channel interest and principal payments from the borrowing majority to the lending minority. In other words, the financial system

---

19 Förster et al., 'Trends in Top Incomes'.
20 Credit Suisse, *Global Wealth Databook 2016*.
21 Michael Kumhof and Romain Rancière, 'Leveraging Inequality', *Finance & Development*, December 2010, 28–31; Thomas Goda and Photis Lysandrou, 'The Contribution of Wealth Concentration to the Subprime Crisis: A Quantitative Estimation', *Cambridge Journal of Economics* 38(2), 301–27.

INTRODUCTION

acts as a mighty transfer system from the bottom up. In order to get to grips with the trinity of private wealth, record debt and rising inequality, we therefore need to understand how the financial system managed to get so large and powerful while at the same time becoming increasingly asymmetrical.

In point of fact, the growing financial assets of the few, which also constitute the growing debts of the many, reflect a restructuring of global capitalism in the second half of the twentieth and the early years of the twenty-first century. This restructuring began with the process of *financialization*: triggered by a relaxation of the rules governing the financial industry and the invention of innovative products, the financial system has, since the late 1970s, become an increasingly attractive place to accumulate capital. More and more capital income has been generated by investing in debt and less and less by investing in labour, industry and other sectors of the real economy. If you want to understand why there is so much private wealth, and why it is so unevenly distributed, you first have to look at why so many financial assets – and hence so many debts – are produced in the first place, and why these investments have become so profitable. Chapter One lays the foundations for this inquiry, pointing to the peculiarity of the driving force behind financialization: credit.[22]

---

22 Obviously, the inequality crisis cannot be explained by any single factor. The economists Anthony B. Atkinson and Branko Milanovic point to the restructuring of labour markets in the second half of the twentieth century as partially responsible for increasing concentrations of income and wealth (Milanovic, *Global Inequality*, 18; Atkinson, *Inequality*, 115ff). The globalization of labour markets – reinforced by the growing technological dependency of production chains – favours highly skilled employees in so-called knowledge-intensive fields, and disadvantages ordinary industrial workers. These views are shared by many institutional economic observers (ILO, *World of Work Report 2011: Making Markets Work for Jobs*, Geneva, 2011; OECD, *Employment Outlook 2007*, Paris, 2007; OECD, *Growing Unequal? Income Distribution and Poverty in OECD Countries*, Paris, 2008; European Commission, *Employment in Europe 2007*, Brussels, 2007; IMF, *World Economic Outlook 2007: Globalization and Inequality*, Washington,

INTRODUCTION

The trinity of growing private wealth, mounting debt and rising inequality testifies to a specific structure within the engine room of capitalism. That structure is all too often underestimated in analyses and critiques, which is another reason for the current lack of rational and targeted solutions to economic crises and new global upheavals. When we talk about capitalism, we generally use the term synonymously with 'capitalist economies'. We regard capitalism as a specific way of organizing economic value creation processes; hence, critical analyses of the system often seek to promote alternative economic models. Champions of digitalization such as Jeremy Rifkin and Paul Mason see new internet technologies as paving the way for post-capitalist value creation processes, as decentralized production and the free sharing of information (such as home 3D printers and the blueprints that tell them what to do) allow products to be made locally, with efficient use of resources and without the constraint of profit maximization.[23] Other anti-capitalist critiques and commentaries argue for non-capitalist value creation processes centring on common ownership, local exchange and giveaway projects, urban self-sufficiency experiments, solidarity networks and many other hope-based alternatives.[24] The problem with this school of thought is its unquestioning equation of capitalism

---

DC, 2007). Piketty (*Capital in the Twenty-First Century*), Joseph Stiglitz (*The Great Divide*, New York, 2015) and many sociologists have explored other causes of the inequality crisis; for an overview, see Steffen Mau and Nadine M. Schöneck, eds, *(Un-)Gerechte (Un-)Gleichheiten*, Berlin, 2015, and Heinz Bude and Philipp Staab, eds, *Kapitalismus und Ungleichheit. Die neuen Verwerfungen*, Frankfurt/New York, 2016.

23 Jeremy Rifkin, *The Zero Marginal Cost Society*, New York, 2014; Paul Mason, *PostCapitalism: A Guide to Our Future*, London, 2015; on the notion of the digital economy as a non-capitalist form of value creation, see Dave Elder-Vass, *Profit and Gift in the Digital Economy*, Cambridge, UK, 2016.

24 See, for example, Silke Helfrich and Heinrich-Böll-Stiftung, eds, *Commons. Für eine neue Politik jenseits von Markt und Staat*, Bielefeld, 2012.

INTRODUCTION

with capitalist economies. At first sight, the use of the term 'capitalist economy' suggests that 'capitalism' and 'economy' are two differentiable concepts. Yet critics then proceed as if the only distinction were between capitalist and pre- or post-capitalist value creation processes; no mention is made of their antithesis. After all, if 'capitalism' and 'economy' are two distinct concepts, then there must be such a thing as *non-economic capitalism*. I attempt to explore this in Chapter Two.

The identification of non-economic – or, to use the slightly more nuanced term adopted later in this book, para-economic (but nonetheless capitalist) – value creation processes is crucial to any analysis (or critique) of the trinity of growing private wealth, mounting debt and rising inequality. After all, the trend towards financialization, which Chapter One breaks down into its various components, is driven by just such a process: the privilege of private banks to create money from nowhere through the extension of credit. This privilege is discussed in Chapter Three. The huge amounts of capital that have driven the rise of the financial system over decades and the accompanying proliferation of debt are not generated by labour, as is sometimes implied in everyday discourse, or by governments, as is commonly assumed, or by central banks, as one often reads in economics textbooks.[25] Nowadays, it is private commercial banks that create the bulk of monetary capital by granting credit 'out of thin air', independently of any government or central bank; all they have to do is tap out a number on a computer keyboard and press Enter. In today's world, monetary capital is generated by a simple keystroke.[26]

The ability of banks to do this without regard to the available supply of capital *property* undermines not only the traditional role of capital owners as the command centre of

---

25 Toby Baxendale, 'Public Attitudes to Banking', The Cobden Centre, 15 June 2010, available at cobdencentre.org.
26 L. Randall Wray, *Modern Money Theory: A Primer on Macroeconomics for Sovereign Money Systems*, New York, 2012, 81.

capitalism, but also the political semantics commonly used to describe and discuss the links between financialization and radically unequal wealth formation. Value creation by banks is an anomaly at the heart of the capitalist system – not because of any failure on their part to act according to capitalist principles, but, on the contrary, because they are able to do so free from the constraints to which actors within economic systems are generally subject. This exceptional situation, in which capital can be created ex nihilo, is what I call 'keystroke capitalism'.[27]

While the first three chapters attempt to explain why debt and private wealth have increased to such an extent over the past quarter of a century, the fourth links this phenomenon to the third element of the triad: the inequality crisis. The aim here is to gain a better understanding of how – that is, through which structures or channels – actors are able to profit from the money creation privilege of private banks. All too often, research on inequality overlooks the fact that, in modern capitalism, economic and *para-economic* distributional effects are mutually interactive. This blind spot also prevents an effective exploration of possible dimensions of change – the subject of the fifth and final chapter of this book. The redistributive state must work to combat the effects of processes set in motion not only by the owners of capital, but also those attributable to its producers – namely, banks. If we want to win this unequal, two-on-one battle, we need to do more than just talk about redistribution: we need to challenge the whole regime of keystroke capitalism.

---

[27] On this concept, see Aaron Sahr, 'Reichtum aus Feenstaub: Das Free-Lunch-Privileg des Keystroke-Kapitalismus', in Bude and Staab, eds, *Kapitalismus und Ungleichheit*, 25–44; Sahr, *Das Versprechen des Geldes. Eine Praxistheorie des Kredits*, Hamburg, 2017.

1
Debt

Imagine you chose to invest 1,000 dollars in gold in 1980: If you had wanted to sell it again twenty-five years later, you could only have done so at a loss.[1] If you had sold your gold in 2020, your investment would have at least slightly more than doubled. Had you invested the same sum in crude oil, it would have bought you almost 30 barrels, whose value in 2005 would have been approximately 1,400 dollars.[2] In 2020, you would have had to sell the barrels for less than 1,200 dollars. If, on the other hand, you had invested your 1,000 dollars in high-performing shares on the American S&P 500 stock market index in 1980, you could have sold them for at least ten times the price in 2005. In 2020, your shares would have earned you almost thirty times your investment. This rise in the price of financial assets is due in large part to a radical transformation of the global economy known as 'financialization'.[3] This term is used in the social sciences to denote a shift in the focus of profit generation from the real to the financial economy from the late 1970s onwards – the emergence of a new dominant accumulation model.[4] Since then, more and

---

1   One troy ounce of gold was worth 615 dollars in 1980 and 445 dollars in 2005; gold price data per Statista.de.

2   OPEC-crude oil price data per Statista.de.

3   A comprehensive review of existing research on this subject can be found in the special issue of the 2015 *Socio-Economic Review* (13[3]) and in Gerald F. Davis and Suntae Kim, 'Financialization of the Economy', *Annual Review of Sociology* 41, 2015, 203–21.

4   Greta Krippner, 'The Financialization of the American Economy', *Socio-Economic Review* 3(2), 2005, 173–208.

more money has been invested *in* and borrowed *from* financial markets, instead of being earned directly through, for example, the production and sale of food or motor vehicles or the provision of services such as hairdressing.

On the financial markets, promises of payment or debts are traded in many different forms.[5] When we talk about financial assets, we are referring not just to basic repayment agreements such as loans for purchasing properties or consumer goods, funding education or company start-ups or investing in corporate and government bonds or shares, but also to payment promises that are enhanced with other elements. Shares, for example, are an entitlement to participate in company profits – a promise of dividends – but they also come with the right to have a say in corporate decisions. Similarly, insurance claims are more than 'just' debts, even though they too are basically payment promises attached to certain conditions. In short, the transformation encapsulated by the term 'financialization' can be understood as the growing ascendancy of debt in modern-day capitalism.

That ascendancy is readily apparent from the statistics: loans and other debt instruments, along with corporate stock, have snowballed from 12 trillion dollars in 1980 to over 56 trillion dollars in 1990, and around 239 trillion dollars in 2015.[6] This means that, between 1980 and 2015, payment promises multiplied much faster than global GDP; in other words, the volume of financial assets has increased most notably *relative to economic output*.[7] Between the end of

---

[5] Susanne Lütz, 'Finanzmärkte', in Andrea Maurer, ed., *Handbuch der Wirtschaftssoziologie*, Wiesbaden, 2008, 341–60.

[6] Kathrin Brandmeir, Michaela Grimm and Arne Holzhausen, *Allianz Global Wealth Report 2015*, Munich, 2015; Susan Lund, Toos Daruvala, Richard Dobbs, et al., 'Financial Globalization: Retreat or Reset?', McKinsey Global Institute, 1 March 2013, available at mckinsey.com.

[7] Although this trend is basically global, it takes very different forms in different economies. See Thomas Philippon and Ariell Reshef, 'An International Look at the Growth of Modern Finance', *Journal of Economic Perspectives* 27(2), 2013, 79.

the nineteenth century and 1970, bank debt in the advanced economies rose from roughly 16 percent to 70 percent of GDP; in 2013, it averaged as much as 140 percent.[8] If we take a look at the World Bank data indicator 'broad money', which, along with bank deposits, includes cash (to a negligible extent), fixed-term deposits and other short- and long-term debt instruments, the same trend becomes clear at a global level: in 1960, financial assets of this kind made up approximately 50 percent of global economic output, compared to a good 133 percent in 2020.[9] Furthermore, in addition to the assets classified as 'broad money', global market capitalization – the value of the world's stock markets – rose from just under 30 percent of total global output in 1975 to around 97 percent in 2015 – and 114 percent in 2019. In short, there is now far more debt relative to economic performance than there was in 1980. This expansion has also been accompanied by an increase in financial sector profits relative to total corporate earnings across all sectors. Or, to put it another way, finance firms are achieving a much higher return on invested capital than industrial companies or non-financial service providers.[10] As such, it is hardly surprising – though important to re-emphasize in this context – that financial sector salaries have risen substantially, and well beyond the general average. In 2000, average earnings in the US financial services industry were around 60

---

[8] Andrew Haldane, 'On Being the Right Size', speech given at the Institute of Economic Affairs' 22nd Annual Series, Bank of England, 25 October 2012, 3, available at bankofengland.co.uk; Philippon and Reshef, 'An International Look'.

[9] World Bank Open Data, The World Bank, available at data.worldbank.org.

[10] Greta Krippner explores this phenomenon in the US; see Krippner, *Capitalizing on Crisis: The Political Origins of the Rise of Finance*, Cambridge, MA, 2011, 31–3. See also Andrew Haldane, Simon Brennan and Vasileios Madouros, 'What Is the Contribution of the Financial Sector: Miracle or Mirage?' in Adair Turner, Andrew Haldane, Paul Woolley, et al., eds, *The Future of Finance, The LSE Report*, London, 2010, 87–120.

percent above the general mean – a difference that did not exist before 1980.[11]

This striking expansion of the finance sector has been driven by a growing demand for financial assets across all sectors of society. In the case of financial products, this demand can (and must) be a two-way proposition: there needs to be someone looking to lend (by making their capital available) and someone looking to borrow – whether to realize a business scheme, afford a dream purchase, invest in education or pay off old debts. The would-be borrower needs instant capital and lacks either the perseverance or the opportunity to save. The would-be creditor – the party cultivating a demand for financial assets – is motivated by the desire to earn money from interest or dividends. In order to understand the phenomenon of financialization, it is therefore helpful to identify which actors have turned increasingly to payment promises as a field of investment, and which have increasingly engaged in borrowing.

Capital Supply

The rising demand for payment promises as a source of investment has come from private households, institutional investors (pension funds, investment funds, insurance companies) and corporations. Most obvious among these are of course private capital holders, among whom increased wealth has led to a greater appetite for investment opportunities. Wealthy private individuals have steadily expanded their share of financial assets relative to that of institutional investors. In the 2000s, that share amounted (globally) to around 41 trillion dollars – more than

---

11 Donald Tomaskovic-Devey and Ken-Hou Lin, 'Income Dynamics, Economic Rents, and the Financialization of the U.S. Economy', *American Sociological Review* 76(4), 2011, 538–59. Even if we look beyond the US and only compare average salaries in the financial services industry with those in academia (as opposed to the lower general average), relative salary growth remains significant: Philippon and Reshef, 'An International Look'.

that of pension funds (28 trillion), insurance companies (20 trillion) or investment funds (26 trillion). In 2007, so-called high net worth individuals (HNWIs)[12] held 14 percent of global debt securities.[13] That the wealthy invest their fortune in shares or bonds is nothing new, and does not therefore account for financialization. However, the growing concentration of investment capital in the hands of a small number of the very rich means that capital gains cannot flow into consumption, but must be invested instead. Accordingly, rising inequality must always be considered as a perpetuating factor of financialization.

As the above figures show, institutional investors are the second biggest driver of the heightened demand for payment promises. Between 1980 and 1995, the capital supply from institutional investors in the US, the UK, Japan, Germany and Canada rose by 400 percent.[14] A key source of this demand is the blue-collar sector. Since the 1980s, many countries in the OECD have seen (at least partially) contributory pension schemes transformed into US-style funds that have to meet pension claims from their own investment income. To echo Panitch and Gindin, this shift signifies the incorporation of workers into the financial system.[15] The prosperity of the postwar decades and hard lobbying by the unions resulted in bulging pension funds, and that capital had to be invested, the bulk of it in shares and bonds.[16]

---

12 People with assets of more than a million dollars.
13 Thomas Goda and Photis Lysandrou, 'The Contribution of Wealth Concentration to the Subprime Crisis: A Quantitative Estimation', *Cambridge Journal of Economics* 38(2), 308.
14 Hans Blommestein, 'The Impact of Institutional Investors on the Financial Markets', in OECD, ed., *Institutional Investors in the New Financial Landscape*, Paris, 1998, 31.
15 Leo Panitch and Sam Gindin, *The Making of Global Capitalism: The Political Economy of American Empire*, London, 2013, 121.
16 R. Della Croce, 'Pension Funds Investment in Infrastructure: Policy Actions', *OECD Working Papers on Finance, Insurance and Private Pensions* 13, 2011; OECD, 'Pension Markets in Focus 2013', available at OECD.org.

The third boost to the demand for financial assets as a source of capital investment has come from non-financial companies. In the world's advanced economies, companies in industry, commerce and non-financial services are increasingly generating their income from investments in financial assets, to the detriment of their actual core business, and hence also to the detriment of investments in real capital such as raw materials, machinery or labour. In the 2000s, the textile manufacturer Nike, for example, managed to increase its income by 1.2 billion dollars. At the same time, Nike's real investments – including spending on raw materials for sportswear production – fell by 12 percent. The gains did not come from the sale of more or better running shoes and functional clothing, but primarily from a 470-percent leap in interest and dividend receipts.[17] GE Capital, the financial arm of the holding company of electronics giant General Electric (founded by the light bulb inventor Thomas Edison), is now the seventh largest bank in the US and responsible for at least half of the group's total profits.[18] In 2004, the automotive group General Motors generated 66 percent of its profits through its in-house bank, and only 34 percent directly from the sale of motor vehicles. Its rival Ford had posted losses for its automotive division that year, but managed to chalk up net profits of over a billion dollars thanks to financial revenues.[19] All these examples are illustrative of a general trend: by 2000, half of all US real-sector investment was already flowing into the country's financial sector, compared with less than a third before 1980.[20] Consequently, investments of this kind have come to play a

---

17 Matthew Soener, 'Why Do Firms Financialize? Meso-Level Evidence from the US Apparel and Footwear Industry, 1991–2007', *Socio-Economic Review* 13(3), 2015, 549f.

18 Krippner, *Capitalizing on Crisis*, 29.

19 Ken-Hou Lin and Donald Tomaskovic-Devey, 'Financialization and U.S. Income Inequality, 1970–2008', *American Journal of Sociology* 118(5), 2013, 1293.

20 Tomaskovic-Devey and Lin, 'Income Dynamics'.

greater role in overall profit generation: indeed, income from financial investments contributed twice as much to the absorbed profits of US real-sector companies in 2007 as it did in 1980.[21] This trend is not unique to the US, although it has been researched in most detail there because the US economy offers the most reliable data. In France, similarly, the share of financial assets relative to the total capital of real-sector companies jumped from around 36 percent in 1978 to nearly 60 percent by 2013. Accordingly, interest and dividend earnings as a proportion of gross operating surplus rose from well below 10 percent in the 1950s to 73 percent in 2008. In other words, only just over a quarter of French real-sector surpluses in that year were actually generated from real production, goods trading or non-financial services.[22]

The Debt Mentality

In order to sustain the demand for financial assets, there has to be a demand for debt. Here, again, we can identify different groups of actors who have increased their borrowing requirement. Firstly, and perhaps least surprisingly, financial companies themselves have raised their leverage more or less continuously, meaning that they have financed more investments with borrowed funds, instead of with their own. I say 'least surprisingly' because investing debts in more debts is the defining business model of a financial services company. Of more interest, therefore, is the fast-growing appetite for borrowing among non-financial actors – that is, real-sector companies, governments and private households. This group shows a marked increase in debt-financed spending since

---

[21] Lin and Tomaskovic-Devey, 'Financialization and U.S. Income Inequality', 1286f.

[22] Ignacio Alvarez, 'Financialization, Non-Financial Corporations and Income Inequality: The Case of France', *Socio-Economic Review* 13(3), 2015, 453f.

1980. The share of funds generated from the sale of products and services, goods trading, wage labour and taxes and then saved for future spending has fallen by comparison with borrowed capital: between 1980 and 2010, the collective debt of these non-financial actors across the OECD doubled relative to gross domestic product.[23] On the one hand, the late 1970s saw the beginning of the 'era of public debt' as slowing growth, falling profits and residual unemployment placed a burden on social security systems.[24] This demand has declined since around the mid-1990s, however, and is dwarfed, above all, by the mounting debt of private households. While corporate debt is increasing by around 50 percentage points, private household debt has doubled.[25] In the US, this process began much earlier, notably with the expansion of credit card networks in the 1960s – the flip side of the increased 'incorporation' of workers into the financial system.[26] The bulk of borrowing in the non-financial sector in OECD countries comes not from governments or companies, therefore, but from consumers.[27] Over the past decades, private household debt has risen significantly not only in proportion to disposable income, but also relative to economic output as a whole – that is, the annually generated sum out of which debt repayments and incurred interest

---

23 Daniel Mertens, *Erst sparen, dann kaufen? Privatverschuldung in Deutschland*, Frankfurt am Main, 2015, 11f.; Stephen Cecchetti, M.S. Mohanty and Fabrizio Zampolli, 'The Real Effects of Debt', *BIS Working Paper* 352, 2011, 5f.

24 Wolfgang Streeck, *Buying Time*, trans. Patrick Camiller and David Fernbach, London, 2017. Krippner, *Capitalizing on Crisis*.

25 Mertens, *Erst sparen, dann kaufen?*, 12.

26 Panitch and Gindin, *The Making of Global Capitalism*, 121.

27 Alan Ahearne and Guntram B. Wolff, 'The Debt Challenge in Europe', *Bruegel Working Paper* 2, 2012, 5; Reuven Glick and Kevin J. Lansing, 'Global Household Leverage, House Prices, and Consumption', *FRBSF Economic Letter* 2010–01, 2010, 3; Guy Debelle, 'Household Debt and the Macroeconomy', BIS, *Quarterly Review*, March 2004, 59–74.

must come.[28] In 2014, private households worldwide were indebted to the tune of 64 percent of nominal global output.[29]

In purely quantitative terms, then, the expansion of financial assets relative to economic output in the world's advanced economies is due to a deepening and widening demand. While lending seems to have become increasingly profitable, so too has the practice of financing one's own spending through borrowing. This double-edged phenomenon can be attributed to a fertile climate for the production of financial assets that has emerged within the OECD since the 1980s. This climate has three components: The first is a change in the relationship between states and their respective financial systems, and indeed in the global financial system as a whole. The second relates to socio-technical innovations within the financial services industry itself, which are radically increasing the flexibility of supply and demand. And the third is a specific appreciation/depreciation dynamic that constantly fuels both demands.[30]

From Control to Protection

The first component of this fertile financial climate is the changed relationship between politics and finance. In the post-war decades, the financial systems of Western economies were shot through with relatively restrictive regulations, particularly by modern standards. Although there were, of course, numerous (and significant) differences between individual

---

28 Aldo Barba and Massimo Pivetti, 'Rising Household Debt: Its Causes and Macroeconomic Implications – A Long-Period Analysis', *Cambridge Journal of Economics* 33(1), 2009, 113.

29 Brandmeir et al., *Allianz Global Wealth Report 2015*.

30 While I outline these components briefly here, a more extensive account of them can be found in Panitch and Gindin, *The Making of Global Capitalism*; Krippner, *Capitalizing on Crisis*; Streeck, *Buying Time*.

countries, in broad terms it is fair to say that the amount of interest banks could pay on their customers' deposits or charge for granting loans was generally limited, transnational capital flows were strictly regulated, currency trading was virtually impossible within the Bretton Woods system of fixed exchange rates, and there were numerous restrictions as to which companies could acquire or produce which assets and which terms should apply to the extension of loans and the structuring of debt instruments in general.[31] Since the early 1980s, these restrictions have been dismantled in virtually all OECD countries.[32] This liberalization process began in the US which, as the holder of the reserve currency – the gold dollar standard – had a determining influence on the (Western) global economy of the postwar period.[33] Scholars have identified two causes of this process. Firstly, the Americans were facing a trade deficit in the 1960s, meaning that more dollars were flowing out of the country than were coming in.[34] There were several reasons for this: the US had a worldwide military presence and operations to keep up, and the central banks of signatories to the Bretton Woods agreement were obliged to maintain dollar reserves in order to keep the 'fixed' dollar exchange rate stable (by buying and selling dollars). Furthermore, American direct investment, particularly in European companies, was growing much faster than investments flowing back into the country (European direct investment in the US was roughly a third as

---

[31] John Williamson and Molly Mahar compare the degree of regulation of the financial system in forty-three countries between 1973 and 1996 in *A Survey of Financial Liberalization*, Princeton, 1998.

[32] See Malcolm Edey and Ketil Hviding, 'An Assessment of Financial Reform in OECD Countries', *OECD Economics Department Working Paper* 154, 1995; for an overview, see Susanne Lütz, *Der Staat und die Globalisierung von Finanzmärkten. Regulative Politik in Deutschland, Großbritannien und den USA*, Frankfurt am Main, 2002; Krippner, *Capitalizing on Crisis*; Panitch and Gindin, *The Making of Global Capitalism*.

[33] Panitch and Gindin, *The Making of Global Capitalism*.

[34] Ibid., 112.

high).³⁵ On top of this, early relaxations of transnational capital flows and the flood of dollars into Europe as a result of the exchange rate system had already led in the late 1950s to the emergence and intensive use of an uncontrolled, dollar-based financial market in London: the so-called Eurodollar market.³⁶ Because transactions promised higher returns here than in domestic systems hamstrung by limited interest rates and administrative constraints, this likewise led to an outflow of US financial capital.³⁷ Actors in the US and European financial markets could now offer their customers unprecedented terms on deposits and loans in their home countries.³⁸ This situation was compounded by a slowing of economic growth in the US and Europe in the late 1960s. The mutual compatibility of rising profits and rising wages made possible by a comparatively high level of labour organization in the prosperous postwar decades – sometimes referred to as the golden age of American capitalism – could now no longer be sustained.³⁹ At first, the powerful unions were able to realize their aspirations, partly due to the existence of virtually full employment in the US, Germany and the UK. However, companies attempted to pass on the burden of rising wages to consumers through price increases, thereby fuelling inflation, and this in turn provoked demands and strike action from a militant labour force. The upshot was a fall in corporate profits in Europe and the US. Between the mid-1960s and 1970, corporate earnings in the US fell by 40 percent, and Europe followed the same trend, albeit with a slightly flatter downward curve.⁴⁰

---

35 Ibid., 113f.
36 Catherine Schenk, 'The Origins of the Eurodollar Market in London: 1955–1963', *Explorations in Economic History* 35(2), 1998, 221–38.
37 Panitch and Gindin, *The Making of Global Capitalism*, 117ff.
38 This development, as Panitch and Gindin demonstrate in *The Making of Global Capitalism*, was also made possible by finance-friendly policies in the US in the 1950s and 60s.
39 Streeck, *Buying Time*.
40 Panitch and Gindin, *The Making of Global Capitalism*.

Companies countered this profit squeeze with higher rates of investment but, because of the downturn, these could no longer be funded with retained earnings. Faced with the double whammy of outflowing financial capital in pursuit of high returns in unregulated markets and an economy in need of capital, the US began to lift the conditions and restrictions on its domestic financial system. Now in a position to promise greater profits than the real economy, the US financial system attracted investment from three global sources during the 1980s: the trade surpluses of export-oriented countries,[41] bulging pension funds from the days of strong growth and labour militancy, and the wealth of private capital investors.[42] Capital flows into the American sector, now leading the way in profit margins, drove more and more countries to improve the friendliness towards capital of their own financial systems. This resulted in something of a locational contest.[43] In virtually all OECD countries, interest rate restrictions were accordingly relaxed, controls demolished, financial contracts granted more leeway and transnational capital transactions simplified.[44] The universal easing of the latter laid the foundations for the rise of tax havens, leading to even more intense locational competition. Tax havens are attractive not only as repositories of wealth smuggled past the tax authorities, but above all as unsupervised debt contract factories. Places with deregulated fiscal and regulatory systems such as Belize, the Isle of Man, the Cayman Islands and Liechtenstein have seen the emergence of offshore financial centres where the business world can exercise its own discretion in contractual and interest policy matters. Since this world is positively defined by its

---

41 Bill Lucarelli, 'Financialization and Global Imbalances', *Review of Radical Political Economics* 44(4), 2012, 429–47.
42 Tomaskovic-Devey and Lin, 'Income Dynamics'.
43 Lütz, *Der Staat und die Globalisierung von Finanzmärkten*.
44 Williamson and Mahar, *A Survey of Financial Liberalization*; Lütz, *Der Staat und die Globalisierung von Finanzmärkten*.

relaxed attitude towards the business transacted there and its minimalist approach to disclosure requirements, one can only guess at the size of its role in global debt production. It is probably safe to assume, however, that a good half of all global debt is linked to a tax haven.[45]

The new flexibility of payment promises in terms of interest rates, repayment terms, payment schedules and so on made possible by the rollback of administrative restrictions meant that a broader demand for borrowing could now be met. This change, together with the liberalization of transnational transactions, presented both investment-seeking capital owners and capital-seeking entrepreneurs and consumers with a vastly expanded range of potential transaction partners. As a result, states faced the constant risk of losing financial capital to other, more lucrative regions, and therefore raced to create the most capital-friendly investment climate. In Germany, this agenda was directly reflected in the wording of the deregulatory legislation, with four 'Financial Market Promotion Acts' passed between 1990 and 2002. Throughout the OECD, the lifting of administrative controls and restrictions accompanied political strategies of positive endorsement designed to increase the profitability of financial investments.[46] To describe the change in the relationship between politics and finance that helped pave the way for financialization as a simple withdrawal of political control or liberalization is therefore an understatement. As a key factor in the fertile financial climate, it should be understood rather as a shift of the political

---

45 Ronen Palan and Anastasia Nesvetailova, 'Elsewhere, Ideally Nowhere: Shadow Banking and Offshore Finance', *CITYPERC Working Paper Series* 1, 2014, 26. For a comprehensive overview of the history, modus operandi and volume of offshore finance, see Ronen Palan, Richard Murphy and Christian Chavagneux, *Tax Havens: How Globalization Really Works*, Ithaca, 2010; Gabriel Zucman, *The Hidden Wealth of Nations: The Scourge of Tax Havens*, trans. Teresa Lavender Fagan, Chicago, 2015.

46 Tomaskovic-Devey and Lin, 'Income Dynamics'; Lütz, *Der Staat und die Globalisierung von Finanzmärkten*.

approach to the financial sector from *control* to *protection*. The relationship between politics and finance over the years of financialization has been characterized not only by supportive legislation, but also by repeated bailouts by governments and central banks.

A turning point in this development was the failure of the privately owned German bank Herstatt in 1974. The German government decided to keep out of the bankruptcy proceedings, with disastrous consequences for the by then internationalized financial system. This crisis prompted a rethink by governments of the OECD countries, after which struggling finance companies found reliable state support once again. Investors began to take it for granted that, in the event of impending insolvency, governments would step in to save at least those companies deemed 'too big to fail', and hence also the smaller satellite firms dependent upon them. The reasoning behind this policy was that there was no other option (particularly for democratic countries) in a financialized and increasingly interdependent global economy; otherwise the whole debt system could collapse.

The expectation that politicians could henceforth be relied upon to intervene whenever the financial system was in crisis had measurable consequences in itself. The anticipation of political support in an emergency encouraged the production of financial assets in normal times. In other words, the assumption that the debt system would be rescued should the banks run into trouble acted like an *implicit subsidy*. Economists at the Bank of England have attempted to calculate the volume of this subsidy and estimate that, between 2002 and 2007, it amounted to an average of 70 billion pounds a year for the world's biggest banks.[47] For the eurozone, the International Monetary Fund (IMF) puts the figure for 2012 at just under

---

47 Joseph Noss and Rhiannon Sowerbutts, 'The Implicit Subsidy of Banks', *Bank of England Financial Stability Paper* 15, 2012.

300 billion dollars.[48] In short, since around 1980, the demand for financial assets as a source of investment and the demand for debt as a source of finance have risen across all spheres of society. An important factor contributing to this twin rise in demand is the changing relationship between politics and finance throughout the OECD: during the initial postwar period, financial systems tended to operate at a local level and were politically embedded and administratively empowered. This changed when declining growth increased the pressure for profitable capital investment, at a time when unregulated international markets were becoming increasingly attractive to the still largely local banks. States became embroiled in a race towards deregulation and began to concentrate more and more on the attractiveness of their financial centres.

Sociotechnical Innovations

A second component of this flourishing financial climate is sociotechnical innovations in the design of financial contracts which revolutionized the possibilities, variations, combinations, size and speed of derivatives in the 1970s.[49] Strictly speaking, derivatives are as old as the financial system itself, which probably dates back as far as the Neolithic Revolution.[50] But they have lately moved centre stage both quantitatively and qualitatively – partly due to increased supply and demand – to the point of becoming the world's biggest market in the early twenty-first century.[51] On the one hand, these transaction volumes have, of course, developed in a liberalized

---

48 IMF, *Global Financial Stability Report*, Washington, DC, April 2014.
49 Edward LiPuma and Benjamin Lee, *Financial Derivatives and the Globalization of Risk*, Durham, 2004.
50 William N. Goetzmann, *Money Changes Everything: How Finance Made Civilization Possible*, Princeton, 2016; Larry Neal, *A Concise History of International Finance. From Babylon to Bernanke*, Cambridge, UK, 2015.
51 Jakob Arnoldi, 'Derivatives, Virtual Values and Real Risks', *Theory, Culture & Society* 21(6), 2004, 28.

environment where finance companies are less constrained in the design of their products. On the other hand, the rise to prominence of derivatives is linked to their function and the nature of payment promises as *risky* social relationships. All debts are subject to a range of risks. Or, to put it another way, there are a range of reasons why they might not be repaid: the borrower could do a moonlight flit; a sudden recession could cause them to lose their job; the company could go into administration and its liabilities could be written off; the start-up could prove not to be such a good idea after all, and so on. Derivatives allow the multitude of individual risks inherent in economic investments to be separated and reorganized so that they can be managed and sold individually. The term is a generic one denoting a variety of contracts promising payments subject to very specific conditions or linked to the performance of certain other payments or indices.

The first of the two main categories of derivatives is that of *futures*. Contracts of this kind fulfil an important function for the real economy. With options and futures, for example, a fee is paid to secure in advance the right (in the case of options) or even the obligation (in that of futures) to conduct future transactions. Futures allow a farmer to fix a certain selling price for his future grain crop at the time of sowing. This benefits him by providing cost certainty and – most important – protecting him from the risk of falling grain prices. That risk is now borne instead by the investor offering the option. With this type of derivative transaction, it is thus possible to individualize the various risks associated with economic activities and sell them separately.[52]

---

52 The possibility of risk segmentation and distribution is also an obvious advantage of the second main category of derivatives: swaps. These can be used to swap cash flows, such as volatile principal payments on a mortgage, against payments that yield less but are pegged to less volatile indices. With credit default swaps, which were especially popular in the 2000s, the default risk on a mortgage could be hedged and traded in return

The popularity of derivatives cannot be attributed solely to the creation of regulatory flexibility, however: it is also based on epistemic and technological potentialities that reset the financial rulebook in the 1970s and 1980s. Derivatives are highly complex payment contracts whose terms – especially their price – are by no means easy to calculate. It was not until the emergence of new probability calculation techniques (notably the 'Black-Scholes' model), the mass migration to the financial industry of mathematicians and physicists (so-called quants) who knew how to apply these formulae, and the invention and popularization of electronic data processing and communication systems that the foundations were laid for the meteoric rise of derivatives.[53] Their functionality catalyzed in equal measure the demand for financial assets and the demand for debt.[54] The risks previously shackled to debt could be fragmented and distributed, and thus ultimately globalized. Indeed, the risks inherent in any financial asset could now be split up and separately hedged. That way, investments could be made ostensibly more secure and duly tailored to

---

for a fee. In 2007, contracts of this kind were used to 'hedge' a good 58 billion dollars' worth of payment promises worldwide, meaning that they were in effect transferred to another party. Financial Crisis Inquiry Commission, *The Financial Crisis Inquiry Report, Final Report of the National Commission on the Causes of the Financial and Economic Crisis in the United States*, New York, 2011, 50.

53 LiPuma and Lee, *Financial Derivatives*, 141ff.; Donald MacKenzie and Yuval Millo, 'Constructing a Market, Performing Theory: The Historical Sociology of a Financial Derivatives Exchange', *American Journal of Sociology* 109(1), 2003, 107–45; Claudia Honegger, Sighard Neckel and Chantal Magnin eds, *Strukturierte Verantwortungslosigkeit. Berichte aus der Bankenwelt*, Berlin, 2010; James Owen Weatherall, *The Physics of Finance: Predicting the Unpredictable: Can Science Beat the Market?*, London, 2013; Joseph Vogl, *The Specter of Capital*, trans. Joachim Redner and Robert Savage, Stanford, CA, 2015; Elena Esposito, *The Future of Futures: The Time of Money in Financing and Society*, Cheltenham, 2011.

54 Arnoldi, 'Derivatives'; Davis and Kim, 'Financialization of the Economy'.

customers' needs.⁵⁵ Creditors could engage in transactions they had previously deemed too risky or opaque, and borrowers could access a wider circle of creditors and hence a cheaper market.⁵⁶ It was thanks to this simplified and extended range of derivatives that financial investments began to appeal to more and more real-sector companies and capital owners – which meant that more lucrative terms could be offered to borrowers too. In this way, under the guise of mathematically and contractually manufactured certainty, high-risk debts could be transferred to creditors around the world, thereby globalizing credit markets and dramatically increasing the field of potential suppliers and customers. As derivatives allowed the risks of individual debts to be itemized and distributed, global networks of transnational dependency began to emerge. Nordic countries bought the risk of price fluctuations

---

55 A key field of sales-boosting derivative products in the 2000s was that of securitization, a process used to turn previously sluggish loans – in particular mortgages, consumer credit and student loans in the US – into globally tradable products. Thanks to the synthetic combination of various types of derivatives, whole clusters of debts could be pooled and the receivables sold wholly or partially as 'credit packages'. This credit package economy allowed the impression to be created – through shrewd exploitation of different disclosure and calculation standards in different jurisdictions, juristic creativity in the drafting of contracts, and the use of actuarial tricks – that the packaged receivables from the original debt pool collectively constituted less risky investments than the original debts themselves. These practices of ostensible 'credit enhancement' (see for example Benjamin H. Mandel, Donald Morgan and Chenyang Wei, 'The Role of Bank Credit Enhancement in Securitization', in Federal Reserve Bank of New York, ed., *The Evolution of Banks and Financial Intermediation. Economic Policy Review* 18(2), New York, 2012, 35–46) were sometimes branded 'alchemistic' (see Efraim Benmelech and Jennifer Dlugosz, 'The Alchemy of CDO Credit Ratings, *NBER Working Paper* 14878, 2009) because they appeared to create certainty – and hence economic value – from nothing.

56 This was particularly important because institutional investors such as pension funds and sovereign wealth funds are often limited to investments above certain security thresholds. See Panitch and Gindin, *The Making of Global Capitalism*, 140; Benmelech and Dlugosz, 'The Alchemy of CDO Credit Ratings', 631.

in South American seafood from sovereign wealth funds and hedged their transactions in turn with Japanese investment banks. German finance companies bought the mortgages of steel workers in the American Midwest from a hedge fund in the Cayman Islands, two thirds of whose capital was owned by a New York bank which likewise invested in the seafood options and guaranteed the German finance companies' hedge fund transactions. These conspicuous examples are only a superficial reflection of how complex the financial system became through the widespread use and creative combination of derivatives. Providing permanent and reliable political support for this densely interconnected and fragile system seemed the only possible strategy. As such, the sociotechnical innovations of the derivatives revolution served to transform the relationship between politics and finance from one of control to one of protection, thereby ushering in the change we have seen in the investment and borrowing climate since the 1980s.

Appreciation and Depreciation Mechanisms

The process of financialization has direct distributional effects which, in turn, contribute to its acceleration. Before proceeding, I should point out that the total annual income of an economy is made up of capital gains (rents, dividends, interest and profits) and earned income. The contribution of the latter to the total income is known as labour's share. In the advanced economies, this share has undergone two marked trends: after World War II, its importance relative to return on capital increased for a time, but has been declining again since the early 1980s.[57] That means that more and more money is going

---

57 Tali Kristal, 'Good Times, Bad Times: Postwar Labor's Share of National Income in Capitalist Democracies', *American Sociological Review* 75(5), 2010, 729–63; Kristal looks specifically at this trend in Australia, Austria, Belgium, Canada, Denmark, Finland, France, Germany, Ireland,

to capital owners, namely landlords, entrepreneurs and creditors, with less and less being paid for labour. The second trend is the internal polarization of the labour share, as mentioned in the Introduction. There, I drew attention to the inequality crisis, one symptom of which is the growing concentration of income at the upper end of the scale, among top earners. In other words, the drop in earned income has not been evenly distributed. Instead, incomes have become polarized: top salaries are rising while average earnings are falling, stagnating or at least developing at a slower rate.[58] In the US, for example, the real wages of the lower-earning half of the population fell by 1 percent between 1978 and 2015, while those of the next highest 40 percent rose by 42 percent and those of the top 10 percent by as much as 115 percent. In the case of the highest-earning 1 percent, the rise in real wages was just shy of 200 percent. This imbalance is evident in Europe as well, albeit on a smaller scale. It is no accident that both trends – the growing importance of capital gains and the divergence of wages – are contemporaneous with the financialization process. Although it would be wrong to pinpoint a single cause,[59] this widening gap is nevertheless closely linked to appreciation and depreciation tendencies that are attributable to – and which effectively perpetuate – the expanding role of financial services within the overall

---

Italy, Japan, the Netherlands, Norway, Sweden, the UK and the US. See also Thomas Piketty, *Capital in the Twenty-First Century*, trans. Arthur Goldhammer, Cambridge, MA, 2014.

58 OECD, *Growing Unequal? Income Distribution and Poverty in OECD Countries*, Paris, 2008, and *Divided We Stand: Why Inequality Keeps Rising*, Paris, 2011.

59 Neither the declining labour share nor the disparity in wages can be attributed exclusively to financialization. For explorations of other factors such as globalization, technical progress and the restructuring of the welfare state, see Piketty, *Capital in the Twenty-First Century*; Anthony B. Atkinson, *Inequality: What Can Be Done?*, Cambridge, MA, 2015; Branko Milanovic, *Global Inequality A New Approach for the Age of Globalization*, Cambridge MA/London, 2016.

economy.⁶⁰ Accordingly, these tendencies should be understood in the sociological sense as mechanisms: they are not just an observable trend, but an engine of financialization, in that they form the causal link between the rising demand for financial assets (among businesses) and the rising demand for borrowing (among private households).

Let us look first at the escalating salaries of the highest-earning 1 percent. Although the growing concentration of income among top earners is partly due to soaring bonuses for sports and show business superstars, it is overwhelmingly the result of salary hikes and incentives for senior executives, managers and CEOs.⁶¹ When we talk about the polarization of earnings, therefore, what we are mainly seeing is a sharp rise in corporate salaries at the executive level, and a much slower growth or even a decline at the 'operational' level. In recent years, the sociology of finance has succeeded in decoding the relationship between financialization and income concentration. There are two forces at work here: an upward 'pull' and a downward 'push'.

The 'pull' stems from superstar CEOs successfully decoupling their remuneration from general market mechanisms. Their pay rises no longer correlate with corporate profits or company size, or with economic growth more generally. Instead, they follow a sector-specific upward spiral which basically operates as follows: managers keep a close eye on salary growth within their own sector or a wider sphere of reference (sometimes called a 'compensation peer group') and instantly demand rises when pay increases take place at other companies.⁶² Supervisory boards generally give in to such demands,

---

60 Petra Dünhaupt, 'An Empirical Assessment of the Contribution of Financialization and Corporate Governance to the Rise in Income Inequality', Institute for International Political Economy Berlin, *Working Paper* 41, 2014.

61 Jerry W. Kim, Bruce Kogut and Jae-Suk Yang, 'Executive Compensation, Fat Cats, and Best Athletes', *American Sociological Review* 80(2), 2015, 299–328.

62 Thomas A. DiPrete, Gregory M. Eirich and Matthew Pittinsky, 'Compensation Benchmarking, Leapfrogs, and the Surge in Executive Pay',

as a reputation for failing to pay their own managers above the average rate would have a negative impact (or so they fear) on the company's market value.[63] Because CEO salaries can no longer be justified by the mechanisms of skill supply and demand or economic trends, but operate, instead, via mutual peer group observation and old-boy networks, the sociologist Sighard Neckel talks of an 'oligarchic closure' of lucrative management positions.[64]

The downward 'push' on income started in the late 1970s, when companies began to derive more and more income from investments in financial assets, while at the same time borrowing more and more in order to fund them. This exerted a twofold pressure on pay structure: firstly, the growing reliance on share issues and loans in order to finance their operations forced companies to focus on a short-term evaluation of their own performance and the business decisions of financial markets. This preoccupation with the markets upon which they ultimately depended (and still depend) for capital, while keeping a watchful eye on any drop in their own share price, is known in sociological research as 'shareholder value orientation'.[65] As a result, operative business became increasingly reliant on share price and the latest corporate credit rating by

---

American Journal of Sociology 115(6), 2010, 1671–712; Kim et al., 'Executive Compensation'.

63 'Targeting below the median [pay] of one's peer group is a public admission that the board has failed in its job of finding the best talent to lead the firm, and the difficulty of attracting top talents would signal to outsiders that the firm is not a desirable employer'. Kim et al., 'Executive Compensation', 303.

64 Sighard Neckel, 'Oligarchische Ungleichheit. Winner-take-all-Positionen in der (obersten) Oberschicht', *WestEnd* 11(2), 2014, 51–63.

65 Julie Froud, Colin Haslam, Sukhdev Johal, et al., 'Shareholder Value and Financialization: Consultancy Promises, Management Moves', *Economy and Society*, 29(1), 2000, 80–110; Paul Windolf, 'Was ist Finanzmarkt-Kapitalismus?', in Paul Windolf, ed., 'Finanzmarkt-Kapitalismus', special issue of *Kölner Zeitschrift für Soziologie und Sozialpsychologie* 45, 2005, 20–57 (English translation available at uni-trier.de).

the banks, and less on long-term sales forecasts for the product itself, be it cars, sportswear, or anything else. In terms of this shareholder value, long-term liabilities such as personnel often proved problematic, but at the same time easy to rectify. So-called human capital is a relatively flexible lever for cutting expenditures and raising profit margins in the short term.

This, then, was the second significant source of downward pressure on wages: Corporate income came to depend less and less on labour, but was itself derived from the financial markets. Reducing these human capital costs became less harmful to a company's market value the more its income hinged on the performance of its own financial investments. The growing share of revenue from financial investments and the corresponding drop in revenue generated directly from the sale of labour-based products such as cars or sportswear can be identified with a migration of bargaining power. The new ascendancy of financial investments meant that that power was now concentrated in the hands of the personnel responsible for such investments, or those who succeeded in taking credit for their success. Consequently, it was analysts and traders, and above all managers and CEOs, who were able to negotiate pay rises. Meanwhile, the bargaining power of those involved in making the product itself – the people beavering away in office cubicles or on assembly lines and shop floors – has declined.[66] The same goes for ancillary industries: when companies cut back on factories, they cut back on cleaning and other services too. Employees who no longer participate as directly in the generation of corporate profits as a 1960s assembly worker at General Motors would have done have little scope to demand more pay. The old call by the unions to down tools has lost its clout.

---

66 Thibault Darcillon 'How Does Finance Affect Labor Market Institutions? An Empirical Analysis in 16 OECD Countries', *Socio-Economic Review* 13(3), 2015, 477–504.

In this way, financialization elevates a small group of top earners while devaluing the majority of the workforce. That this phenomenon is one of the drivers of rising inequality is plain to see: the key, however, is to identify the mechanism behind it. The growing popularity of debt-financed investments is forcing companies to keep an eye on creditor assessments of their performance. The more important investments in financial assets become to corporate profits, the more they affect those assessments. This results in a loss of bargaining power on the part of the majority doing the operative work. Consequently, managers can push through their spiralling pay rises, decoupled as they are from market mechanisms, without resistance.

Furthermore, sociological research in the first decade of the twenty-first century has demonstrated, under the label 'privatized Keynesianism', that this mechanism is also linked to the lion's share of the debt boom – that of private households.[67] The liberalization of the financial system and the rise of innovative forms of capital (backed by political agendas) created an outlet for the consumption and investment aspirations of the blue-collar majority impacted by the forces of devaluation. The credit offers made cheaper by the greater range and ease of supply were the only 'defensive strategy'[68] protecting those hit by stagnating or falling real wages against a threatened loss of status. In the quest to maintain living standards and purchasing power, borrowing became an all-purpose tool, driven by consistently low interest rates and

---

67 Colin Crouch, 'Privatised Keynesianism: An Unacknowledged Policy Regime', *The British Journal of Politics and International Relations* 11(3), 2009, 382–99; Brigitte Young, 'Vom staatlichen zum privatisierten Keynesianismus. Der globale makroökonomische Kontext der Finanzkrise und der Privatverschuldung', *Zeitschrift für internationale Beziehungen* 16(1), 2009, 141–59; Streeck, *Buying Time*.

68 Neil Fligstein and Adam Goldstein, 'The Emergence of a Finance Culture in American Households, 1989–2007', *Socio-Economic Review* 13(3), 2015, 575.

enticing repayment terms.[69] In this sense, the rise in private debt should be understood at least partly as a consequence of the appreciation/depreciation mechanism that has continued to fuel the financialization process.

#ownership

The transformation of capitalism in the late twentieth and early twenty-first centuries is unmistakable. Over this period, more and more capital has been accumulated by lending, whether to businesses promising dividends in return, to insurance companies or investment funds offering annuities in old age or emergency, or to conventional borrowers undertaking to repay the sum with interest. This trend reflects an underlying dynamic: for one thing, the conditions for loan agreements were improved in terms of flexibility of design, the ability to set interest rates and repayment schedules, and the geographical location of the contracting parties, thanks both to changing political regulations and administrative structures and the sociotechnical possibilities of the derivatives revolution. Such possibilities vastly expanded the range of options offered by the financial system, thus allowing the development of new demand potentials such as highly specific risk preferences or hedging standards. In addition, derivatives made it relatively easy to invest in economies and markets in faraway regions or hitherto poorly accessible economic sectors. Lending and borrowing became simpler, more lucrative and more flexible. This made investment in finance an attractive proposition for businesses. As they turned increasingly to the stock and credit markets for capital (also and especially for their financial operations), spending on employees below executive level

---

69 Barba and Pivetti, 'Rising Household Debt'; Lucarelli, 'Financialization and Global Imbalances'; Goda and Lysandrou, 'The Contribution of Wealth Concentration', 313.

(investment management companies aside) was accordingly squeezed. This contributed in no small part to the phenomenon of wage divergence – the increasing concentration of the diminishing labour share among high earners. Enticed by favourable terms and glittering promises of consumer goods, a majority of the employees partially or wholly excluded from these pay rises took to the capital markets themselves in order to 'defend' their living standard or realize long-held house-buying and retail ambitions, thereby sparking a huge rise in household debt.

However complex and (hopefully) conclusive a picture even this brief history of financialization has managed to present, it is still lacking a key component. Businesses have got into more debt in order to invest in the debts of others. Governments have earned less and borrowed more. The bulk of labour income has barely risen, or (as in the US) has even declined, yet consumers have borrowed more and more to fund their expenditure. As a result, world debt has risen to almost 320 percent of global economic output.[70] But where did all this money come from? What was the source of this capital and, moreover, of these increases that have outpaced economic growth to such an overwhelming extent? Where did the money lent to all the private households, governments and businesses come from? The answer to this question does not lie in the superficial transformation of the accumulation models themselves. To get to the bottom of it, we need to descend to the engine room of capitalism.

---

70 Lund et al., 'Financial Globalization'.

II

Ownership

The Lannister family is a powerful force on the fictional continent of Westeros; its territory, safeguarded by ancient oaths, archaic traditions and a military presence, harbours the largest gold reserves in the region. As readers of the book series made famous by the popular TV show *Game of Thrones* will know, the Lannisters use this wealth to bribe allies and raise vast armies of mercenaries, equipping them with weapons and armour. Thanks to the gold mines, the family members even become creditors of the ruler, who is prey to legendary extravagance. Over the course of the story, the Lannisters quickly rise to the peak of their influence on the continent, acceding to the throne of the Seven Kingdoms. Later in the story, however, viewers learn from the head of the family, Tywin,[1] that the gold mines have in fact been dry for years. At this turning point in the narrative, the House of Lannister's power begins to crumble: the family loses allies, the throne gradually slips from its grasp and it suffers military and personal defeats. In the Lannisters' case, power and gold are closely connected. In contrast to some of the other great ruling families in this fantasy epic, their power is not built primarily on honour and friendship or a shared proto-national idea, nor does it stem from the location and nature of their territory: It is strictly *economic power*, which is transferred to the political system by means of bribery,

---

[1] *Game of Thrones*, season 4, episode 5, 'First of His Name', directed by Michelle MacLaren, aired 4 May 2014, on HBO.

lending to influential actors and mercenary armies. Such conversions of economic to political power (and vice versa) are also common in many parts of our own world, whether through corruption, favours in exchange for campaign donations or revolving door arrangements whereby CEOs of successful companies temporarily enter the political establishment and then return (often after deregulation) to the free market. This and other variants of the relationship between economics and politics are not the point at issue here, however: The career of House of Lannister is notable for something much more fundamental. The story describes economic power as something that derives from possession; the Lannisters' *capacity* to act results from their *ownership* of valuable property. It is the quantity of gold they have *at their disposal* that constitutes their potency as actors. Accordingly, the family's power begins to collapse once their gold reserves run out and the source of valuable property is exhausted. This may seem a trivial observation, but it is not. The theory of economic agency based on ownership is reflected not only in the fantasy world of a successful TV series, but also in the axiomatic concepts of capitalist theory in our own world. Property and economic power, 'ownership' and 'capacity', are almost always perceived as fundamentally interconnected.[2] As we shall see, however, this theory blinds us to a source of capital and wealth accumulation important to both financialization and the inequality crisis. For this, we must turn for a moment to the theory that will help us unlock the engine room of capitalism as a whole.

---

2 Note that 'property' or 'ownership' are not used here as legal terms, but as practical ones. They refer to the power of disposal over existing resources, or, more broadly, already accumulated economic value.

From System to Practice

Usually, the term capitalism is used synonymously with 'capitalist economy'.[3] As such, it is generally regarded as a distinctive economic system, a web of institutions that evolved between the sixteenth and nineteenth centuries in Europe, thereby replacing the previous economic system of feudally organized production, distribution and consumption of goods and services.[4] There is no perfect consensus on the precise organization of this system, but the customary definitions have many elements in common. These typically include a dynamic arising from the individual right to private property and its disposal; market competition; the mass production of goods; a social structure based on the division of labour; the principle of free labour; rational calculation technologies and the appropriate cognitive capacities; and an institutionally embedded credit system through which to fund investments.[5] Capitalism is assumed to be the sum of all the above – a system made up of many components. My purpose here is not to weigh in on the contents of this checklist, but to briefly highlight the problems of such a systemic approach (however we choose to define the precise components). Thinking in systemic terms imposes certain analytical constraints that hinder a detailed

---

[3] Geoffrey Ingham, *Capitalism*, Cambridge, 2008, 2.

[4] For example: Richard Swedberg, 'The Economic Sociology of Capitalism: An Introduction and Agenda', in Victor Nee and Richard Swedberg, eds, *The Economic Sociology of Capitalism*, Princeton, 2005, 3–40; Ingham, *Capitalism*; Miguel Centeno and Joseph Cohen, *Global Capitalism: A Sociological Perspective*, Cambridge, UK, 2010; Paul Swanson, *An Introduction to Capitalism*, New York, 2013; Geoffrey M. Hodgson, *Conceptualizing Capitalism: Institutions, Evolution, Future*, Chicago, 2015; Jens Beckert, *Imagined Futures, Fictional Expectations and Capitalist Dynamics*, Cambridge, MA, 2016.

[5] This mainstream definition is reconstructed by Stephen G. Marks from a broad range of literature in *The Information Nexus: Global Capitalism From the Renaissance to the Present*, Cambridge, UK, 2016 (wherein he also proposes an entirely different definition of his own).

study of financialization, capitalism and inequality – and for two reasons, the first of which was described in the Introduction.[6] The premise that capitalism is necessarily economic (the same goes for the term 'capitalist society') means that capitalism and the economy are perpetually associated in our minds. As we shall see in the next chapter, however, it would be wrong in some respects to describe the credit system as economic, yet it is unquestionably capitalist. To conceive of capitalism as a specifically economic system is to ignore this para-economic form of capitalism; as such, the systemic approach is guilty of a serious omission. Besides, the common tendency to systematize the concept makes it tempting to visualize the capitalist economy as a kind of container encompassing everything that happens within it. Such a definition is based on a somewhat 'monolithic' view of economic capitalism (as Dave Elder-Vass puts it in his critique of Karl Marx), because all actors and economic activity after the birth of the capitalist system are classed as capitalist, in the sense that they operate 'within' a capitalist economy.[7] Thus, companies, markets and states automatically become capitalist companies, markets and states,[8] although it is not immediately clear what is to be gained by labelling them as such. The use of systemic terminology implies that the mere fact that the relevant actors or activities are part of, or subjects of, the system, and can therefore be measured with the same theoretical yardstick, tells us all we need to know about them (hence Elder-Vass's reference to the *monolithic* nature of systemic theories). For one thing,

---

6 My argument here broadly echoes Dave Elder-Vass, *Profit and Gift in the Digital Economy*, Cambridge, UK, 2016; Thomas Welskopp, *Unternehmen Praxisgeschichte*, Tübingen, 2014; and Welskopp, 'Zukunft bewirtschaften, Überlegungen zu einer praxistheoretisch informierten Historisierung des Kapitalismus', *Mittelweg 36* 26(1), 2017, 81–97.

7 Elder-Vass, *Profit and Gift in the Digital Economy*.

8 See Leo Panitch and Sam Gindin, *The Making of Global Capitalism: The Political Economy of American Empire*, London, 2013; Beckert, *Imagined Futures*.

this can incline us to overlook differences, diversity, coincidences and contradictions.[9] Above all, however, it lessens the analytical granularity of the concept because everything that happens within the capitalist era – that is, the period of time for which this institutional framework exists – is subsumed under the phenomenon of capitalism. As a result, necessary distinctions can only be made by incorporating further assumptions. If capitalism is formally defined as a system, a web of institutions, it becomes a kind of container for countless different behaviours, relationships and ways of making sense of the world. In order to study the triad of growing private wealth, mounting debt and rising inequality, we need to step outside this container logic. Not everything that happens in modern economies is capitalist in nature, nor is everything that happens within capitalism economic.[10] We need a finer differentiation tool.

This critique comes from a school of thought that sees society as a web not of institutions and actors, but of social practices. Without delving too deeply into the vexed debate surrounding this concept, the following argument builds on the same idea – namely, that social constructs such as 'the economy' or 'capitalism' are complex arrangements of social practices. They can be understood as ordered patterns of social activity or interaction – in other words, established 'tendencies to act in a certain way'.[11] The social world consists of countless patterns of activity that have (to a greater or lesser extent) become ingrained. The best way to avoid the problems associated with the systemic approach is to proceed from the basic premise that capitalism and economics likewise constitute, in broad terms, specific ways of doing certain things.[12]

---

[9] For more of this critique, see Elder-Vass, *Profit and Gift in the Digital Economy*; Welskopp, 'Zukunft bewirtschaften'.
[10] On this point, see Elder-Vass, *Profit and Gift in the Digital Economy*.
[11] Ibid., 99.
[12] Welskopp, 'Zukunft bewirtschaften', 87.

Accordingly, the terms 'economics' and 'capitalism' should, at best, be understood as substantivizations of activities that are better described in verb form – that is to say, as practices.[13] My purpose, therefore, is to establish what makes certain ways of doing things capitalist practices or, to echo Thomas Welskopp, what – beyond the 'purely temporal circumstance' that they take place within a certain period (and hence within an institutional framework) – 'adequately characterizes' a variety of social activities as capitalist.[14] Since this requires us to distinguish *economic* from *para-economic* capitalist practices, however, we must first answer the question of what qualifies particular modes of social interaction as economic practices in the first place. Happily, this essay's concern with the present relieves us of the obligation to offer an ahistorical definition. To refine the terms of the question, therefore: Which aspects of the modern capitalist economy are in fact *economic* and which are *capitalist*?[15]

Economic Practices

Amid the near-endless variety of definitions of economics, two central themes emerge that are crucial to the identification of keystroke capitalism: scarcity and exchange. Both of these are inherent in the ancient Greek concept *oikonomía*. In ancient economic philosophy, we find the notion of what Joseph Schumpeter calls an 'embryonic' economy, which has

---

13 On this, see Sören Brandes and Malte Zierenberg, 'Doing Capitalism', *Mittelweg 36* 26(1), 2017, 3–24.

14 Welskopp, 'Zukunft bewirtschaften', 87.

15 The following remarks are not intended as a lesson in archaic forms of economic organization. The theory that we are currently witnessing a partially para-economic form of capitalism does not mean that the 'economy' part of a 'capitalist economy' no longer operates like the early forms of economic management, nor is it undermined by the possibility of alternative forms of economy. My point is rather that the banking system negates contemporary and popular definitions of economics.

survived in terms of its key aspects into the present-day theoretical discourse of modern economies.[16] In its first sense of 'housekeeping', *oikonomía* means the management of the scarce resources and (less scarce) needs of a community: in other words, the organization of material reproduction in conditions of scarcity. Although there are some traditions in which the definition of economics does not explicitly refer to scarcity, it can nevertheless be regarded as the basic principle of economic discourse. Scarcity as a defining characteristic of economic practice also features prominently in sociology.[17] The reason for this emphasis is that, from a sociological perspective, scarcity is not merely synonymous with the finiteness of resources and time. Nor does it mean a shortage of something: rather, it is a 'specific form of social organization'.[18] Here too, then, we can think of it as a certain mode of social interaction. As such, scarcity is not a passive condition governing our actions (as many economists would probably understand it), but a particular kind of behaviour. The most precise definition of that behaviour is probably Niklas Luhmann's notion of mutually exclusive access.[19] Scarcity means accessing goods that others are likewise capable and desirous of accessing – and in such a way as to preclude any further access to those goods. Therefore, if we hold scarcity to be the first characteristic that identifies a specific way of doing things as an economic practice, then economic practices are those which involve competition for access to a given resource.

---

16 Joseph A. Schumpeter, *History of Economic Analysis*, London, 1954, 60.

17 On this, see Aaron Sahr, *Das Versprechen des Geldes. Eine Praxistheorie des Kredits*, Hamburg, 2017, 145–59.

18 André Orléan, *The Empire of Value: A New Foundation for Economics*, Cambridge, MA, 2014, 88.

19 Niklas Luhmann, *Die Wirtschaft der Gesellschaft*, Frankfurt/M., 1994; Dirk Baecker, *Wirtschaftssoziologie*, Bielefeld, 2006; Aaron Sahr, 'Von Richard Nixon zur 1000 000 000 000-$-Münze. Kreditgeld als politische Verknappungsaufgabe', *Mittelweg 36* 22(3), 2013, 4–31.

Secondly, successful household management depends, according to both Aristotle and Xenophon (the two primary sources of economic theory from the ancient world), upon interaction with other households – a practice that can be described as an exchange of property.[20] Anyone who owns property can exchange it; in fact, in societies based on the division of labour, they are obliged to do so, as household management depends on exchanging surpluses from one's own production with surpluses from another. In essence, therefore, economic theory is to this day a theory of exchange, and the same applies within sociology.[21] The classic articulation of this second principle in the modern age is that of Adam Smith, who famously defined economic activity as arising from the human propensity to 'truck, barter and exchange'.[22] As the father of modern economic theory, Smith describes the commercial society already evolving around him in the seventeenth century as one where owners of property interact in markets in order to exchange goods and services for money, each with a view to their own profit. The owner of any commodity, be it their labour, a manufactured product or

---

20 Dirk Baecker, 'Wirtschaft als funktionales Teilsystem', in Andrea Maurer, ed., *Handbuch der Wirtschaftssoziologie*, Wiesbaden, 2017, 163–80.

21 For economic theory, see Schumpeter, *History of Economic Analysis*; Dudley Dillard, 'The Barter Illusion in Classical and Neoclassical Economics', *Eastern Economic Journal* 14(4), 1988, 299–318; David Graeber, *Debt: The First 5,000 Years*, New York, 2011; for examples from recent sociological research, see Milan Zafirovski, 'Economic Action', in Milan Zafirovski and Jens Beckert, eds, *International Encyclopedia of Economic Sociology*, New York, 2011, 165–74; Andrea Maurer and Gertraude Mikl-Horke, *Wirtschaftssoziologie*, Baden-Baden, 2015, 31; for a detailed reconstruction, see Frank Hillebrandt, *Praktiken des Tauschens. Zur Soziologie symbolischer Formen der Reziprozität*, Wiesbaden, 2009; for a general overview, see Sahr, *Das Versprechen des Geldes*. The degree to which economic sociology is rooted in exchange theory is evident especially in its focus on the market as an object of study – on this, see Jan Sparsam, *Wirtschaft in der New Economic Sociology. Eine Systematisierung und Kritik*, Wiesbaden, 2015.

22 Adam Smith, *An Inquiry into the Nature and Causes of the Wealth of Nations*, London, 1776, 15.

Economic Practices

simply money, has to find someone who is in need of that particular thing.[23] The exchange of goods produced from finite resources, then, is a second recurring theme of economic theories.

The thread that links these two themes (modern economics as a practice based on scarcity and modern economics as a practice based on exchange) is the right of ownership. The concept of ownership, meaning the exclusive right to possess, use and dispose of a thing,[24] occupies a key role in modern economic theory. To be precise, social scientists traditionally tend to conceive of economics as a practice of interaction between owners and non-owners.[25] Once again, Niklas Luhmann has probably put this most succinctly. In modern economies, scarce resources and goods may only be accessed legitimately by their owner. Therefore, the reproduction of scarcity through competing access to finite things only becomes effective through the right of ownership. In Luhmann's view, it is this that distinguishes modern economies from premodern ones: the fact that ownership has replaced violence, chance or social status as the basis for economic agency by allowing legitimate access according to the scarcity principle.[26]

This embedding of economic agency in ownership also applies to the second constant in our definition of economic practices: that of exchange. Anyone with ownership rights to a given item of property is entitled to do two things, which are effectively two sides of the same coin: they can exclude others from accessing it, or not. In other words, they can dispose of their property by making distributional decisions, such as whether to transfer it to someone else. Exchange, then, is a

---

23 Ibid., 24ff.
24 Bernhard Schäfers, 'Eigentum', in Bernhard Schäfers and Johannes Kopp, eds, *Grundbegriffe der Soziologie*, Wiesbaden, 2010, 57.
25 See Sahr, *Das Versprechen des Geldes*.
26 This does not rule out the existence of social practices whereby finite resources can be legitimately accessed on a different basis.

reciprocal, voluntary granting of access to scarce goods. In modern economies, property can only be 'lawfully' acquired 'by transfer from another owner'.[27] According to Luhmann, ownership is therefore synonymous with the capacity to act, in the sense of being able to initiate an exchange – that is, to motivate another person to participate in a simultaneous voluntary transfer of property. In economic terms, Luhmann argues, 'to have' (*haben*) is 'to be able' (*können*).[28]

The practice of accessing scarce resources for the production and/or exchange of goods is one in which agency depends on the accessor's ownership of the resources and the status of the exchanging parties as both owners and non-owners vis-à-vis each other. What makes a given practice an economic practice, therefore, is that it involves accessing scarce commodities, and that the capacity to do so derives from ownership, or, rather, from the difference between ownership and non-ownership. In this context, money is deemed the most desirable form of property,[29] because it is a universal medium of exchange: Because of its universal desirability, any other form of property included in the economic system by the assignment of a price can, in theory, be accessed by handing over money. As such, money is seen to represent the ultimate 'capacity to get things done': Anyone who *owns* enough money has the *capacity* to obtain any other saleable (scarce) form of property.[30] For the purpose of the following reflections, then, economic

---

27 Niklas Luhmann, 'Der Ursprung des Eigentums und seine Legitimation. Ein historischer Bericht', in Werner Krawietz, Antonio Martino and Kenneth Winston, eds, *Technischer Imperativ und Legitimationskrise des Rechts*, Berlin, 1991, 46.

28 Niklas Luhmann, *Rechtssystem und Rechtsdogmatik*, Stuttgart, 1974, 63. Strictly speaking, it is of course not just ownership that constitutes economic agency, but the difference between ownership and non-ownership. This applies whenever one party has something that the other wants (and does not have) and when a voluntary transfer is possible and an involuntary one is not, or at least not legally (according to the right of ownership).

29 On this specific point, see Sahr, *Das Versprechen des Geldes*.

30 Geoffrey Ingham, *The Nature of Money*, Cambridge, 2004, 4.

practices are those in which scarce resources are turned into property which is, in turn, exchanged against the scarce property of another party. In short, economic practices always entail competing access to property, whereby capacity is contingent upon ownership.

Capitalist Practices

That 'capitalism' is all too often equated with 'capitalist economics' is evident from the common tendency to view capitalism in itself from the perspective of ownership. Indeed, the concept of (private) property is the cornerstone of many capitalist theories. Despite numerous differences in the details, only a few of which can be discussed here, many definitions of capitalist economics revolve around the basic idea of private individuals deploying their wealth with the aim of increasing it. As such, they habitually resort to the simple formula proposed by Karl Marx to describe this phenomenon: the capitalist invests a previously accumulated sum of money (M) in commodities (C), either by purchasing them directly or – and this is the nub of Marx's theory – by purchasing resources, machinery and labour. The money is invested in commodities not for the purpose of consumption, however, but in order to sell them at a profit (M'). In Marx's thinking and beyond, capitalism reduced to its simplest definition is M-C-M' – meaning, the aim of capital owners is to increase their capital.[31] Capitalist practices, therefore, are characterized firstly by a specific objective (*telos*), namely that of moneymaking, or, to

---

31 Karl Marx, *Capital*, Volume I, trans. Samuel Moore and Edward Aveling, first published Moscow, 1887, Part II, Chapter 4. A similar definition of capitalism can be found in James Fulcher, *Capitalism: A Very Short Introduction*, Oxford, 2004; Luc Boltanski and Eve Chiapello, *The New Spirit of Capitalism*, trans. Gregory Elliott, London, 2006; Klaus Dörre, Stephan Lessenich and Hartmut Rosa, *Sociology – Capitalism – Critique*, trans. Jan-Peter Herrmann and Loren Balhorn, London, 2015; Swedberg, 'The Economic Sociology of Capitalism'.

use the classical terminology, capital accumulation. For anyone interested in an analytical differentiation of economic and capitalist practices, this means removing ownership and competition for finite resources from the classical formula. Paradoxical as it may seem at first sight, capitalist practices are then no longer the result of decisions made by asset holders on the basis of (capital) ownership, but are instead geared entirely to the teleology of profit. As such, they are practices entailing the 'systematically projective deployment of resources ... in speculative anticipation of an outcome ... exceeding the volume of the deployed resources'.[32]

This objective is only the first of the two components necessary for a solid sociological definition of capitalism, however. For the activity of speculation to be possible at all, there needs to be an expectation of success. In order for the invested funds to swell their owner's capital assets, therefore, the investment practice must be integrated into concrete social complexes that add the earned profit to those assets. M can be turned into M' because of the existence of profit appropriation mechanisms that ensure that the bulk of the return on capital investment accrues to those already in possession of capital (not as a result of any normative preference, but simply as empirical fact). It is the existence of such identifiable channels that perpetuates the asymmetry between the small number of decision makers and beneficiaries, and the many who, while they may not lose out *entirely*, certainly benefit *less* from capital deployment decisions. This structural asymmetry was what Karl Marx had in his sights when he talked about private ownership of the means of production.[33] His notion of capitalist or bourgeois production referred to a very specific socioeconomic formation in which the appropriation

---

32 Welskopp, 'Zukunft bewirtschaften', 88.
33 For the account of Marx's argument that follows, see Emery Kay Hunt and Mark Lautzenheiser, *History of Economic Thought: A Critical Perspective*, New York, 2011, 3–8.

of profit is essentially linked to wage labour: The means necessary to produce saleable goods through the deployment of labour are privately owned – and by a social minority located among the bourgeoisie.[34] The means of production are the ownable means (land, machinery, patent rights and so forth) by which the goods necessary for the reproduction of the population are produced through labour. Private ownership of the means of production allows the few to do what those who only have their labour to offer cannot: namely, to appropriate the difference between the costs of production and the proceeds from sales (M').

In today's world, however, the business of asset production and profit generation is only loosely related to the deployment of labour power. That much is clear from the sheer volume of debts and derivatives highlighted in Chapter One. Whether these are produced in their tens or tens of thousands is a matter almost entirely divorced from the factor of wage labour, and the same is true of digital products. Capitalism scholars are therefore well advised to put the 'obsessive identification of capitalism with wage labour' resolutely behind them.[35] What remains, however, is the second aspect of Marx's concept of the means of production – and that is as crucial as ever to capitalist practices. The means of production are not just the equipment that allows resources to be turned into goods through labour, but also the social arrangements that allow their owner to legitimately claim the profits from that process. Here again, therefore, I would adopt Elder-Vass's suggested characterization of this element of capitalism not as 'private

---

34 The term 'means of production' in its traditional Marxist sense is inextricably linked to the labour theory of value (see Marx, *Capital*, Vol. I, Part 2, Ch. 6, Sale and Purchase of Labour-Power; Karl Marx, 'Wage Labour and Capital', trans. Frederick Engels, original pamphlet published 1891). One writer who has drawn prominently on a definition harking back to the concept of surplus value extraction is Wolfgang Streeck; see 'How Will Capitalism End?', *New Left Review* 87, 2014, 48.

35 Elder-Vass, *Profit and Gift in the Digital Economy*, 45.

ownership of the means of production', but as complexes of *appropriative practices*.[36] Thus, the analysis of a capitalist economy requires us to consider profit-driven capital investments that are embedded in asymmetric complexes of appropriative practices. Appropriative practices are those which transfer economic benefits to individuals and groups of individuals. This may sound a rather loose, abstract definition, but it relates to very concrete things such as employment contracts, for example. An employment contract assigns a proportion of corporate income to a wage earner. By the same token, shares assign a proportion of corporate income to a shareholder in the form of dividends. Elder-Vass's use of the term 'appropriation' is analytically neutral here, meaning the direction or channelling of economic benefits; no value judgement is implied.

Nevertheless, practices such as the issuing of employment contracts or shares do not exist in a vacuum, but are part of larger complexes involved in the direction of economic benefit. Thus, the income arising from an employment contract depends on taxation and redistribution policies, just as the purchasing power of that income depends on general price trends, and so on. Similarly, the value of shares is of course contingent not just on the company's economic performance, but also on factors such as the existence and nature of trading platforms; legal norms and legal realities governing company shares and their valuation, sale and implementation; tax rates and state taxation powers; accounting procedures, and much more besides. This complex of multiple ways of doing things may be configured in such a manner that significantly more economic benefits are directed towards certain individuals or groups of individuals over a longer period of time and via identifiable mechanisms. If this can be demonstrated empirically, we can speak of asymmetric

---

36 Ibid., 101–14.

appropriative complexes. Without putting a name to it, Chapter One discussed something of this kind in reconstructing the concept of financialization as a mechanism that tends to devalue the majority of the workforce and elevate top earners and asset holders. In Chapter Four, the impact of the financial industry as an appropriative complex will be examined in more detail.

#capacity

Based on the above, we can now differentiate between economic and capitalist practices before going on to delineate a para-economic zone in the next two chapters. What makes modern capitalist economies *economic* practices is the fact that they are based on competing access to finite resources. In other words, they allow scarce resources to be turned into capital assets which can then be exchanged for other assets – a process that can be described as a mutual granting of access to property. In economic practices, access to scarce resources is governed by ownership rights: property begets capacity, or the power to act. What makes modern capitalist economies *capitalist* practices, on the other hand, is the fact that the resources in question are accessed for a specific purpose – namely to achieve returns and increase one's own wealth – and that this wealth accumulation is embedded in appropriative complexes whereby the investor is systemically more likely to succeed than to fail. This is not to imply that all transactions within a given geographical area or era are part of a capitalist economic system, or to suggest that all transactions, or even all investments, are only ever concluded or undertaken for profit. It simply means that a practice is only defined as capitalist if it entails the activities outlined above, as a specific 'way of doing things'. In capitalist practices, individuals act with a view to increasing their private wealth, and those who are most successful at appropriating the returns from such activities are those with existing capital.

These attempts at conceptual differentiation lead us back, finally, to the Lannisters on the fictional continent of Westeros. In the epic narrative of *Game of Thrones*, as soon as House of Lannister begins to fall following the exhaustion of the gold mines, a new power comes to the fore: the Iron Bank of Braavos. This name is dropped repeatedly from the beginning of the series, but its relevance to the story only gradually becomes apparent. Not only does the crown owe vast sums to this bank, but the Lannisters too have got into debt in their attempt to slow down the decline of their influence and so hide their weakness from the other ruling families of the Seven Kingdoms. Viewers and readers encounter Westeros at a point in its history in which a new kind of power is emerging that is distinct from the old, property-based economic power of the Lannisters: the Seven Kingdoms are witnessing the dawn of an age of banking – and with it the power of credit. Unfortunately (or fortunately in terms of narrative suspense), neither the books nor the series offer much information about the modus operandi of the Iron Bank. Thankfully, we know considerably more about lending conditions in the real world, since we too live in an age of banking, and we too have seen the banks usher in a new kind of agency or capacity that allows the existence of capitalist practices which cannot at the same time, or at least not in any real sense, be deemed economic practices. In today's world, bank loans are para-economic practices – an anomaly at the heart of the capitalist economy which I call 'keystroke capitalism'.

III

Capacity

The engine of capitalism runs on a single fuel: bank debt. Capitalist economies are monetary and transactional economies, and the universal means of payment – money – exists (nowadays at least) purely in the form of bank debt. From a legal point of view, the bank balances drawn on for most payment transactions are sums which the bank *owes* to the account holder. This is, in effect, also true of cash. The colourful notes we use to pay for things become money not simply by being printed, but because the central bank enters them on the debit side of its balance sheet. Consequently, when we speak nowadays of a monetary economy, we are referring to money in the sense of 'circulatable liabilities'.[1] This currency, in the form of cash or book money, is used to fund purchases and investments, pay taxes and settle debts. When someone transfers money from one bank account to another, the bank's debt to them is reduced – their balance goes down and the recipient's balance goes up. In the same way, borrowed sums such as student loans are settled by paying back sufficient 'circulatable liabilities', or credit. As such, banks can be said to form the infrastructure of capitalism for three reasons. Firstly, the money used to pay for things in a transactional economy consists of bank debt. Secondly, the lion's share of transactions is organized and managed by the banking system. And thirdly (a point that is, alas, aired far too little), banks produce the

---

[1] Udo Reifner, *Das Geld. Recht des Geldes, Regulierung und Gerechtigkeit*, vol. 3, Wiesbaden, 2017, vol. 3, 1.

means of payment (money) in the form of circulatable liabilities. Banks create new money by granting credit or buying assets: that is to say, they are *capital producers*. This chapter will consider the conditions under which that production takes place – conditions which have to do with the nature of money itself. In this context, money is the name for a social relationship consisting of credit (that of the account holder) at one end and debt (that of the bank where the account is held) at the other. To give material form to this relationship within a functioning political and economic order, all it takes is a piece of paper (a banknote) or a tiny unit of computer memory (a bank account). Debts are codified (contractually documented) numbers representing a promise of payment. One of the most fascinating features of modern capitalism is the fact that accounting techniques can be used in this way to create assets and make profits. I am not talking here about the use of number-crunching tricks to find loopholes in already loosely drafted tax regulations. My point is rather that the very act of entering credits and debits on a balance sheet – in effect, the act of writing itself – can generate capital and thereby contribute to its accumulation. On one level, this observation is simply stating the obvious: we routinely pay for our weekly shop by writing our name on a piece of paper or tapping in a code at the checkout that makes the figure in our bank account go down and the figure in the wholesaler's go up. On another level, however, we can understand the act of writing as an alternative means to solvency which falls below the radar of ownership theory as formulated by mainstream approaches to the study of economics and capitalism, but is nevertheless crucial to the capitalist dynamic. The fact is, banks now have the *capacity* to make payments without the constraint of *ownership*.

Written Values

Capitalism is a transactional economy and the medium of those transactions – money – exists these days in the legal form of bank debt. But how does this bank debt arise? Or, to put it another way, how do banks create money? To answer this question, it helps to take a brief look at the historical context. Before the existence of banks, earned, inherited or stolen wealth could be exchanged or hoarded. With the invention of modern banks around the thirteenth century, however, and their rapid spread across Europe from the fifteenth century onwards, a systematic and institutionalized method of saving developed.[2] Saving differs from hoarding in that it entails the transfer of (private) wealth to a contractual partner (the bank) who can then invest the money and so maintain the economic cycle.[3] In other words, saving involves debt; by saving, we become a creditor of the bank. The foundations of these now commonplace social technologies were laid (in Europe) in the high and late medieval period, when the 'commercial revolution' – the emergence of diverse and complex continental and intercontinental trading relations – fuelled the demand for efficient payment systems. Allowing for a little historical simplification, we can think of the payment system customary at that time in roughly the following terms: When we talk of money in the medieval context, we are talking primarily of precious metal (gold or silver) coins which were produced more or less by the state, or at least by politically authorized minters. The business of mining and processing the precious metal and minting the

---

[2] As I am dealing with a modern theory here, I begin at this point, though a comprehensive history of banking would start much earlier. For the earliest forms of banking organization, see David Graeber, *Debt: The First 5,000 Years*, New York, 2011, and William N. Goetzmann, *Money Changes Everything: How Finance Made Civilization Possible*, Princeton, 2016.

[3] See Niklas Luhmann, *Die Wirtschaft der Gesellschaft*, Frankfurt/M., 1994.

coins was elaborate and struggled to keep pace with the increasing commercialization of Europe and the steady expansion of Eurasian and European–African trade during this period. Consequently, there were frequent bullion famines. This benefited the money changers who, since their first appearance around the thirteenth century, had been offering specialist services that could replace coins in monetary transactions. They would often sit on benches at long tables counting coins and entering the amounts in ledgers; such, at least, is the etymology of the word 'bank' (from 'banc', meaning 'bench'). This period saw the emergence of a range of cashless (meaning, in this case, coinless) payment methods. One method favoured within the Central European trade fair system – a series of large, regularly occurring transregional trade meetings – was the bill of exchange: a promise in writing to pay out a given sum at a specified time or on demand and as such, a functional prototype of modern-day contracts between bank account holders and their credit institutes.[4] It was through contracts of this kind that the economic shift towards debt as a medium of exchange was able to take place. Medieval merchants began to take their stocks of coins, which were heavy and risky to transport, to these early bankers, who would enter the equivalent sum in their books in return. Paper receipts could also be issued bearing the promised amount, and these could be changed back again at other locations within Europe's growing network of money changers. If the investors wanted their gold deposits back, they would present the receipt and pay the money changer a small safekeeping fee. It was here, then, that the practice of saving was effectively established: coins were deposited with private banks which then issued paper receipts (banknotes) or simply recorded the amount as book money – that is, money that existed in the same cashless form as most of our money today

---

4 Hans-Jörg Gilomen, *Wirtschaftsgeschichte des Mittelalters*, Munich, 2014.

(as in a current or checking account, for example). This intrinsically valueless book money (also referred to as 'substanceless' credit and essentially consisting of nothing more than numeric information) could then be used for buying and selling just like the precious metal currency itself. Credit and banknotes had become anonymously transferable, meaning they could be exchanged for coins by whoever owned them.[5] It no longer mattered whether you or someone else had brought the substanceless credit into being by depositing the cash with a money changer: you could simply use the anonymized receipt as a means of payment instead of withdrawing the coins. In this way, bank liabilities became circulatable, and debt became a medium of exchange. This arrangement was not yet on a par with the modern banking system, however. Although the money changers' paper receipts and book entries could be used as a currency, their production had to be (pre-)*financed* by savings deposits. These deposits consisted of valuable property that the banks were unable to produce themselves. It was only through this property (in the form of savings) that they acquired their capacity to act (by issuing credit).

Eventually, European merchants of the high and late medieval period became accustomed to doing business based on bank debt instead of precious metal coins. As the historian Gabriela Signori writes, 'Debt was just as ubiquitous in the conceptual and real world of the premodern period, afflicted as it was by coin shortages, as it is in the modern world of banks and credit cards.'[6] Bankers transferred valuable property

---

5 See Geoffrey Ingham, *The Nature of Money*, Cambridge, 2004; Christian Postberg, *Macht und Geld. Über die gesellschaftliche Bedeutung monetärer Verfassungen*, Frankfurt am Main, 2013.

6 Gabriela Signori, 'Einleitung', in Gabriela Signori, ed., *Prekäre Ökonomien, Schulden in Spätmittelalter und Früher Neuzeit*, Konstanz, 2014, 7. One reason for the ubiquity of debt in this period was the simple fact that large sections of the population had no regular income; Peter Schuster, 'Soziale und kulturelle Aspekte des Schuldenmachens', in Signori, ed., *Prekäre Ökonomien*, 17–34.

from one owner to another by simply raising and lowering their respective bank balances. In the increasingly important world of finance, property no longer changed hands by means of physical transportation, but 'by a simple stroke of a pen'.[7] For this reason, early transactions of this kind in Venice were called *banchi di scritta*, referring to the long table at which the movements of money and debts were recorded. This written method of asset distribution has shaped our economy to this day, as any shopper signing a receipt or entering a number in a payment terminal will appreciate. Just as in medieval times, the act of writing causes the bank's debt towards the seller to rise and its debt towards the buyer to fall. The same thing happens when you sign your name or enter your PIN at the checkout in order to transfer an amount from your account to the retailer's. But to return to the Middle Ages: people became gradually less inclined to use and hence withdraw the deposited stocks of gold or silver as book entries and paper receipts proved to be functional and reliable ways of managing day-to-day business, and the banks were thereby able to become producers. They now issued more paper receipts, this time on credit, meaning that the *promised* amounts of gold or silver exceeded the actual physical reserves. The early 'scriptural banks' of Venice already allowed their customers 'to overdraw their account by creating book money that existed purely in the form of numbers in the bank's books'.[8] This gave rise to the 'fractional reserve' principle, which is still commonly used in analyses of the modern banking system. Bank debts serving as a medium of exchange could be created with a stroke of the pen provided the bank's customers – the account holders or creditors – could be confident of being able to access the gold or silver reserves *if necessary*. As long as only a few customers

---

[7] Michael North, 'Banking: Middle Ages and Early Modern Period', in Joel Mokyr, ed., *The Oxford Encyclopedia of Economic History*, vol. 1, Oxford, 2003, 223.

[8] Gilomen, *Wirtschaftsgeschichte des Mittelalters*, 92.

actually redeemed the bank's payment promises by requesting the written sums in gold or silver, it did not matter that these reserves only amounted to a small 'fraction' of the total written sum owned by its collective clientele. If this trust in the bank's ability to pay out in gold and silver was shaken, a bank run could ensue, which meant that all reserves were used up and the bank had to declare insolvency because there was no way that it could settle all of its debts at once.

This fractional reserve system was progressively expanded with each new variant of the precious metal standard during the nineteenth and twentieth centuries. From now on, the gold or silver reserves were deposited in the vaults of a central bank, with whom individual retail or commercial banks then held accounts. In other words, the commercial banks' 'reserves' were now merely payment pledges on the part of the central bank, meaning that any trader, company or employee depositing money with a bank no longer received a promise of silver or gold, but a promise of a promise. In systems with a precious metal standard, only the central bank owns assets that are more than just written numbers. Yet these too constitute only a small part – a fraction – of the central bank's total funds, which in turn make up the fractional reserve of a much larger volume of book money held by private commercial banks. The book money in the current and savings accounts used for day-to-day transactions remains a liability of the commercial bank. The difference is that it is no longer a promise of gold or silver, but a promise of payment by the central bank, which we carry around with us in the form of banknotes. The circulatable liabilities became mere claims on claims.

The last attempt to establish a monetary system of this kind was the postwar Bretton Woods agreement, which introduced a further layer to the network of payment promises in the majority of Western countries. Under this system, the gold standard was expanded into a gold dollar standard. Only the US Federal Reserve Bank issued book money, which signified – at least formally – a promise of gold assets. From then on, the signatory states to this agreement produced their own, substanceless currencies based on fractional dollar reserves, and the private commercial banks in turn – through the extension of credit – created further book money which, although only a gold debt in the most abstract sense, was nevertheless a functioning credit-based currency. Due to a series of misfortunes, this network was dissolved in 1973 and replaced with the global money system that still exists today. Nowadays, there is no longer a (systemically critical) gold deposit held by a particular central bank, but there are still 'reserves'. I use the word in quotes because they are very different from the precious metal reserves of previous centuries. Today, central bank reserves consist of substanceless book entries just like those in a private bank account. Economists describe this as a 'fiat money system', meaning one in which all currency, including reserves, consists of nothing more than written bank debts. This development has changed capitalism more fundamentally than is generally acknowledged.

Distributive Institutions

In the previous chapter, we saw that the definition of economics as a social practice in which capacity derives from ownership and is limited by scarcity is one that chimes with the prevailing assumptions of sociology. The next question to answer is where modern-day banks fit into all this. In mainstream economic and sociological theory, banks are considered an inconspicuous part of economic practice.[9] By inconspicuous, I mean that they are generally assumed to be, in essence, ordinary economic actors, not unlike goods traders. As a rule, banks are conceived of as intermediaries or distribution

---

9 For more detail on this, see Aaron Sahr, *Das Versprechen des Geldes. Eine Praxistheorie des Kredits*, Hamburg, 2017, 141–96.

machines which collect (finite) capital stocks in the form of savings deposits and distribute them. In other words, they borrow funds from capital owners, who thus become depositors, and lend them out to debt-happy consumers or investors, who in turn become borrowers.[10] In the laconic register of former German finance minister Wolfgang Schäuble, 'One person saves money; another needs money. This has to be organized. It's called banking. It's as simple as that.'[11] In an interview with the *New Yorker*, the Nobel Prize–winning economist Eugene Fama is similarly succinct: 'People who get credit have to get it from somewhere'– namely, from a capital holder or depositor.[12] This popular distribution theory understands the banks' agency as economic power in the sense described in Chapter Two – as deriving from property or ownership, that

---

10 On this model and its dominance, see Zoltan Jakab and Michael Kumhof, 'Banks Are Not Intermediaries of Loanable Funds – And Why This Matters', *Bank of England Working Paper* 529, 2015, and Richard Werner, 'Can Banks Individually Create Money Out Of Nothing? – The Theories and the Empirical Evidence', *International Review of Financial Analysis* 36, 2014, 1–19. For an example of its use in economics, see Franklin Allen and Douglas Gale, 'Financial Intermediaries and Markets', *Econometrica* 22(4), 1023–61; Sudipto Bhattacharya and Anjan V. Thakor, 'Contemporary Banking Theory', *Journal of Financial Intermediation* 3(1), 1993, 2–50; Michael A. Klein, 'A Theory of the Banking Firm', *Journal of Money, Credit and Banking* 3(2), 1971, 205–18; Paul Krugman and Robin Wells, *Economics*, New York, 2005; Frederic S. Mishkin, *The Economics of Money, Banking, and Financial Markets*, Harlow, UK, 2013. Economic sociology tends likewise to subscribe to the tradition of distribution theory – see for example Linda Stearns and Mark Mizruchi, 'Banking and Financial Markets', in Neil Smelser and Richard Swedberg, eds, *The Handbook of Economic Sociology*, Princeton, 2005, 287; Mitchel Abolafia, 'Financial Markets', in Jens Beckert and Milan Zafirovski, eds, *International Encyclopedia of Economic Sociology*, London, 2006, 278; Susanne Lütz, 'Finanzmärkte', in Andrea Maurer, ed., *Handbuch der Wirtschaftssoziologie*, Wiesbaden, 2008, 341; Gerald F. Davis and Suntae Kim, 'Financialization of the Economy', *Annual Review of Sociology* 41, 2015, 204; Hans-Joachim Klein, 'Geld', in Johannes Kopp and Bernhard Schäfers, eds, *Grundbegriffe der Soziologie*, Wiesbaden, 2010, 83.
11 Wolfgang Schäuble, *Stern* No. 48/2008, 20th November 2008, p. 53.
12 John Cassidy, 'Interview with Eugene Fama', *New Yorker*, 13 January 2010, available at newyorker.com.

is, possessing previously accumulated valuable assets. It assumes this agency – meaning the capacity to make investment decisions – to be contingent on prior withdrawals of scarce assets and deposits of saved capital. In this respect, therefore, social scientists commonly regard the banking and finance system as a 'normal' economic practice.

For the greater part of this potted history of modern banking, distribution theory makes obvious sense. The money changers needed savers to supply them with a stock of precious metals before they could write new book money into existence in exchange for a promise of repayment from capital-seeking customers, and so produce real, useable money on credit. Even in this 'penstroke economy', however, banks were still dependent on the possession or appropriation of funds which they could not produce themselves and which were needed to underpin their own book money production as a fractional reserve – partly to prevent a run on the bank by deposit holders, and partly because a minimum reserve was (and still is) compulsory in many countries. This is why the inclusive approach that sees banks as ordinary players on the economic stage still appears valid, even in the eyes of many mainstream economists.[13] The argument goes as follows: private banks have an account with their central bank containing a credit balance that they cannot generate themselves by writing down a few numbers. They need this credit not just because the regulations say so, but because it enables them to meet their obligation to hold a minimum reserve, and hence access cash that they are likewise unable to print themselves. Cash and the non-cash book credit of the banks together make up the central bank's monetary base, and private commercial banks can convert one form of central bank credit into another. The

---

[13] Hanno Pahl, 'A Little Apparatus Called IS-LM. Steuerungsvisionen des hydraulischen Keynesianismus', in Walter Ötsch, Katrin Hirte, Stephan Pühringer, et al., eds, *Markt! Welcher Markt?*, Marburg, 2015, 91f.; see also Sahr, *Das Versprechen des Geldes*, 33ff.

reason they need to do so is because their in-credit customers are entitled to exchange that credit for cash – that is, to change private commercial bank credit into central bank credit. When you or I withdraw money from a cashpoint, we are effectively converting money that our bank can produce itself into money that it cannot, and which it therefore has to *access* from elsewhere. Hence the widespread hypothesis that, because of the scarcity of central bank reserves, private commercial banks compete for access to this central bank money, and their own money production is therefore subject to a liquidity risk. Put simply, when banks grant their customers a new, previously nonexistent book credit, they are exposing themselves to the risk of that customer making a cash withdrawal even though the amount in the bank's possession has not (yet) increased commensurately. In short, although banks can create new book money from nothing by simply granting credit, this increases their reserve requirement. If a commercial bank does not have enough central bank money to meet the minimum reserve stipulations or the needs of its customers, it can top it up in one of three ways. It can wait for an injection of book money or cash from customers (via cash deposits or transfers to its accounts); it can borrow surplus reserves from other banks on the interbank market; or it can request a loan from the central bank, which then places new credit in its account. Consequently, mainstream theory assumes that private commercial banks only use their capacity to create book money 'out of thin air'[14]

---

14 This expression is commonly used in the literature; see, for example, Ingham, *The Nature of Money*; L. Randall Wray, *Modern Money Theory: A Primer on Macroeconomics for Sovereign Money Systems*, New York, 2012; Josh Ryan-Collins, Tony Greenham, Richard Werner, et al., *Where Does Money Come From? A Guide to the UK Monetary and Banking System*, London, 2011; Mary Mellor, *Debt or Democracy. Public Money for Sustainability and Social Justice*, London, 2016; Ann Pettifor, *The Production of Money: How to Break the Powers of Bankers*, London, 2017. Werner's 'Can Banks Individually Create Money Out Of Nothing?', 16, refers rather more poetically to 'fairy dust' in this context.

by offering credit once they have acquired reserve funds with which to underpin that credit. Those who subscribe to this view therefore regard banks as intermediaries or capital distribution machines which, although they have more money to 'distribute' (by producing it on credit) than they have coming in, still remain dependent on inflows. Before they can generate their own funds, banks first have to receive valuable assets that they are unable to create for themselves. If private banks generated money without securing the necessary reserves in advance, they would risk depriving themselves of their own commercial basis. Therefore, the production of written book money by private banks relies on previously accumulated capital, acquired through savings deposits and interbank or central bank loans.[15] The logical consequence of this is that central banks can control the money supply simply by limiting or increasing the availability of reserves as they see fit – or so we are led to believe by what the socioeconomist Joseph Huber calls 'grey theory'.[16]

Capital Producers

In practice, however, as many critical economists, sociologists and other social scientists have pointed out, things are very different: in fact, they are exactly the other way round. It is not the central banks who are the prime movers, by generating the funds necessary for reserves and thus enabling the private banks to operate: On the contrary, the latter are entirely independent of any central bank in their decision-making. This much was conceded by the Deutsche Bundesbank in its monthly report of April 2017, in a departure from previous

---

[15] For specific examples of this, see Mishkin, *The Economics of Money*, 389.

[16] Joseph Huber, 'Monetäre Modernisierung. Vom Giralgeld zum Vollgeld', in Klaus Kraemer and Sebastian Nessel, eds, *Geld und Krise, Die sozialen Grundlagan moderner Geldordnungen*, Frankfurt am Main, 2015, 294.

assessments of its own importance: 'It suffices to look at the creation of (book) money as a set of straightforward accounting entries to grasp that money and credit are created as the result of complex interactions between banks, non-banks and the central bank. And a bank's ability to grant loans and create money has nothing to do with whether it already has excess reserves or deposits at its disposal.'[17] This point is demonstrated particularly forcefully by a field experiment conducted by the economist Richard Werner. He obtained a loan (albeit instantly repayable) from a local bank in order to monitor what went on in the bank's books after the loan had been extended. Once the loan application had been approved, the sum appeared in a specially created account for the beneficiary; afterwards, the loan was marked as paid off and the sum disappeared again. When Werner asked the head of the bank what role reserves played in this process, he was told: 'In connection with the extension of credit to you ... I am pleased to confirm that neither I as director ... nor our staff checked either before or during the granting of the loan to you whether we keep sufficient funds with our central bank ... We also did not ... undertake any transfers or account bookings in order to finance the credit balance on your account.'[18] In other words, private banks do not even consider whether they have sufficient deposits to cover loans: they simply create new money on credit if they think borrowers are likely to be able to pay them back.[19] This works because the account holder's entitlement to cash arising from this self-generated credit no longer poses any real risk to the banks. Indeed, central banks – contrary to the assumptions of the distribution theory model – have been successfully meeting orders for new cash

---

17 Deutsche Bundesbank, *Monthly Report – April 2017*, 15, available at Bundesbank.de

18 Werner, 'Can Banks Individually Create Money Out Of Nothing?', appended letter translated from German.

19 Pettifor, *The Production of Money*, 25.

for decades.[20] In order to understand the economic dynamic of our time, it is therefore crucial to recognize that the dependencies between private commercial banks and their central banks are the exact opposite of those assumed by the distributive model. The ability to pump more money into the economy through increased investment and spending depends not just on central banks 'printing' more of it, but also on the demand for, and sanctioning of, private bank debt. It is this debt that creates a demand for central bank money in the first place – a demand which is in practice invariably met. Consequently, central bank money should be regarded not as the prerequisite, but as the result of private money creation.[21] Private banks are the proactive 'initiators of money creation'.[22] Nowadays, they can supply the economy with any amount of funds if the demand from borrowers is there and they deem it lucrative enough.[23] In this way, they have emancipated themselves from capital ownership: They do not need to possess pre-existing valuable assets in order to pay. As we saw in the words of Wolfgang Schäuble and Eugene Fama, the assumption stubbornly persists among economic experts that 'deposits ... are lent to other customers in the form of loans.

---

20 'It is important to understand that central banks currently place no limit on cash made available to private commercial banks to satisfy a loan application.' Ibid., 26.

21 '[R]ather than the central bank controlling the amount of credit that commercial banks can issue, it is the commercial banks that determine the central bank reserves.' Ryan-Collins et al., *Where Does Money Come From?*, 7; cf. Jakab and Kumhof, 'Banks Are Not Intermediaries of Loanable Funds'.

22 Postberg, *Macht und Geld*, 129. 'The reality is that banks ... create as much or as little fiat money as they see fit ... Through their proactive ... money creation, banks generate monetary facts, of which the central bank is then retrospectively *obliged* to refinance a fraction.' Huber, 'Monetäre Modernisierung', 295. (Translation by Sharon Howe.)

23 'Commercial banks are now in the position to supply whatever volume of credit to the economy their borrowers demand.' Basil J. Moore, *Horizontalists and Verticalists: The Macroeconomics of Credit Money*, Cambridge, 1988, 4.

Yet the banking sector no longer needs deposits.'[24] It is no longer the case, as Fama assumes, that you have to get credit 'from somewhere' – that is, from a lender of some kind; nowadays, it comes from 'nowhere', at the touch of a button. If you pay for a purchase with your overdraft, a debit will appear in your account, but the credit transferred to the seller's account has not been taken from anyone else – it has been created from scratch. All it takes to approve a consumer loan for the purchase of a car (or the purchase of a share by a bank) is to enter a number on a computer keyboard. 'A keystroke', writes the economist L. Randall Wray, 'turns that [entered number] into "reality"'; in other words, 'keystroke money' is created.[25] The bank 'has *no need* to pre-finance its loan'.[26] Modern-day capitalism can only be understood, therefore, by recognizing that saving is now 'a consequence, not a cause, of such lending'.[27] Today, private commercial banks create deposits from nowhere: they no longer *finance* loans by distributing funds, but actually *originate* them, to adopt Robert Unger's distinction.[28] This process involves no mediation at all between saved assets and would-be borrowers. The 'capacity' of banks, meaning their ability to make investment decisions, does not depend on them having valuable assets at their disposal.

#appropriation

Chapter Two argued that a capitalist economy is one that is characterized by economically capitalist practices. In capitalist practices, people act with a view to increasing their private

---

24 Huber, 'Monetäre Modernisierung', 293.
25 Wray, *Modern Money Theory*, 64; Mellor, *Debt or Democracy*, 109.
26 Robert Unger, 'Traditional Banks, Shadow Banks and the US Credit Boom: Credit Origination Versus Financing', *Bundesbank Discussion Paper* 11, 2016, 9, emphasis added.
27 Jakab and Kumhof, 'Banks Are Not Intermediaries of Loanable Funds', 4.
28 Unger, 'Traditional Banks'.

fortune, and those most successful at appropriating the returns from such activities are those who already own capital. In economic practices, scarce resources are accessed on the basis of ownership rights. Inside the engine room of our socio-economic world, however, banks are able to finance investments with capital they create themselves, without regard to the available stocks of valuable assets – or to central bank provisions. In terms of money creation, central banks are reactive actors. Private banks, not the central bank, perform the keystroke that dictates how much money there is. Credit no longer has to be financed, as it is not limited by scarce resources. As such, private bank credit should be regarded as an *anomaly* of the capitalist economy: Banks grant credit to make a profit even though the capacity to make such investment decisions is not constituted by previously accumulated disposable assets. In other words, banks have a *para-economic privilege* allowing them to issue money without having to *own* (or even borrow) any in the first place. This practice of being able to pay at the touch of a button, without any prior funds and while making a profit, is what I call 'keystroke capitalism'. In Chapter Two, we noted that capitalist practices are defined not only by the actors' desire to accumulate capital, but also by the fact that those most successful at it – that is, those who reap the biggest profits – are those who have already accumulated capital in the past. In order to understand the concept of keystroke capitalism, we therefore need to consider the specific appropriative complexes surrounding the money creation privilege. Put simply, it is time to examine the question of who actually profits from the keystroke money of private banks, and how. This is not just a matter of inventing flashy terminology. The practice of creating money out of nothing is emphatically a privilege. Yet privileges and exceptions are, strictly speaking, only considered justified in democratic societies if they are of benefit to the community. Such, at any rate, is the opening premise of the Declaration of the Rights of Man and of the Citizen adopted during the French Revolution in 1789. When it comes to assessing the community benefit of keystroke capitalism, however, there are good grounds for cautious scepticism.

IV

Appropriation

No one can deny the ingenuity of chemistry teacher Walter White in the face of challenging circumstances. Despite his precarious job situation and lack of health insurance, the protagonist of the hit series *Breaking Bad* is only momentarily thrown off course by his cancer diagnosis. With the Damocles sword of unaffordable treatment costs and an uncertain outcome hanging over him and his family, he soon comes up with a creative response: he applies his skill and expertise with chemical substances – largely dormant in his job as a high school teacher – to synthesizing the drug methamphetamine. In fact, he produces a drug of such unrivalled quality that he suddenly finds himself in possession of something he previously lacked: economically exploitable capital. With this capital comes the prospect of accumulating enough money to finance his cancer treatment and, moreover, to support his family should the treatment fail. The rest of the series follows White's attempt to establish via methamphetamine what Chapter Two, using Elder-Vass's terminology, referred to as appropriative practices: the socially embedded value creation and distribution processes that turn economic returns into private wealth. Despite its obvious connotations, the term 'appropriative' should not be interpreted as a value judgement: in the sense intended here, even welfare benefits or earned income are appropriations of returns from various value creation and distribution processes. Within capitalism, according to our sharpened definition in Chapter Two, such processes are established and maintained for the purpose of generating positive returns – the first component of the concept – and they are embedded in complexes of appropriative practices which tend to channel the bulk of the returns towards those with existing assets. In contrast to the notion of autonomously managed households commonly found in economic texts, the sociological perspective works on the principle that the generation of personal wealth invariably, and necessarily, results from arrangements of appropriative practices and their effects – in short, from appropriative complexes. In *Breaking Bad*, we have a textbook example of this. For Walter White, it is not enough to invent a uniquely high-quality product: in order to derive economic benefit from his invention, he has to organize a complex value creation process embedded in various appropriative practices. For example, he is obliged to find a partner (Jesse Pinkman) who can give him access to distribution channels. Pinkman's hegemonic knowledge allows him to direct a share of the market profits from the drug's sale to himself. But a not inconsiderable proportion also lands in the pockets of the established dealers, who use brute violence to deny White access to the street-corner marketplaces. Furthermore, White is forced to launder the illegally obtained money – that is, to legalize it as allegedly regular income via a shell company which he has to purchase and maintain. As a result, the company staff absorb some of the sale proceeds, and – by way of business taxes and social security contributions – so does the state (and so on). We should resist the impulse to see the income of the established drug dealers, the wages of the shell company staff and the remuneration of Jesse Pinkman as a parasitic drain on capital flows that should by rights have accrued to only one of the actors involved: Walter White, the originator of the pure meth. While it is the chemistry teacher's technical genius and skill that make this value creation process possible in the first place, he is able to appropriate the returns as capital only after anchoring the process in various appropriative practices. In empirical reality, value creation processes must be embedded in highly intricate complexes of appropriative practices of this kind in order to come to fruition – and that goes equally for legal (and less morally repugnant) economic models. To put it bluntly, in a capitalist economy – even on the legal side of value creation – you cannot make money out of something without others getting in on the act. Although all economic value creation processes are, by definition, embedded in such appropriative practices, in the case of capitalist practices – as we established in Chapter Two – they are arranged, at a higher level of abstraction (macroscopically), in complexes whereby the capital-owning minority benefits the most. Before we can describe a particular historical situation within a particular sector of society as capitalism, we need to be able to demonstrate the asymmetry of its appropriative complexes. To validate the diagnosis of 'keystroke capitalism', therefore, we need to examine the extent to which this embedding can also be demonstrated for *para-economic* value creation processes driven by bank credit. Accordingly, this chapter deals with the very simple question of who benefits from the act of creating money out of nothing. It does not do this, however, in the microscopic detail that *Breaking Bad* brings to its depiction of the hero's attempts to establish and maintain a value creation process for methamphetamine. Such description would exceed the scope of this book, and it is more important for a proper assessment of keystroke capitalism to adopt a broader, macroscopic perspective and consider the para-economically driven financial system as an appropriative complex in its own right. As it is, existing research on capitalism rests on the widespread assumption of a dualism between two key complexes which influence all value creation processes within a capitalist economy, while the para-economic complex remains unexplored.

The Dualism Within the Political Economy

As a rule, capitalism research assumes that legal wealth and wealth accumulation in the Western world of 'democratic capitalism' arise from one of two contexts of activity which follow different logics and generate different expectations.[1] These two contexts can be understood as two distinct macroscopic appropriative complexes, meaning arrangements of numerous practices and regulations which direct economic assets and income streams and derive private wealth from value creation processes according to their respective principles. It is neither necessary nor possible to go into the precise structure of these complexes here (as in the fictional example of Walter White); the point is rather to extend the dualistic framework we commonly use when attempting to account for the asymmetrical wealth distribution we see today. The first (and widely regarded as primary) appropriative complex is that of capitalist markets, where capital owners exchange raw materials, goods and labour for money. Here, income is generated and capital accumulated by selling your property at a higher price than you paid for it. These more or less free mutual exchanges result in a distribution of wealth, but an unequal one, as there is no principle or mechanism for ensuring that everyone ends up (by a given date) with exactly the same amount as before. To demand this of a market would, moreover, be absurd: For one thing, the word 'market' is no more than a collective term for the countless acts of exchange that take place, and which often have little to do with the desire to achieve parity. Anyone who forks out for the latest smartphone knowingly and voluntarily increases the wealth of the manufacturer, who will have invested significantly less in its production. How much customers are prepared to pay for

---

[1] Wolfgang Streeck, *Buying Time*, trans. Patrick Camiller and David Fernbach, London, 2017.

a product seldom bears any relation to what the company has spent making it – what matters is how keen customers are to own a particular phone, regardless of what that desire is worth to them and what prompted it. In themselves, therefore, markets are far from conducive to equitable distribution, and it is not hard to see why inequality researchers – as represented here by the sociologist Steffen Mau – put the main emphasis on 'market-generated disparities'.[2]

Not all income and wealth stem from myriad buying and selling decisions, however: The state, too, intervenes in these market outcomes. As a rule, capitalist markets are subject to taxation and, as such, the democratic redistributive state constitutes the second main appropriative complex of democratic societies.[3] Three examples of the use of this appropriative dualism spring to mind here: firstly, the historian Jürgen Kocka and the political scientist Wolfgang Merkel refer to a 'structural division of power between market and state', or 'between economic resources and political power', in modern democratic societies.[4] Similarly, in his book *Capitalism*, the sociologist Geoffrey Ingham argues that modern societies are characterized by a specific power distribution between private economic processes and state institutions.[5] And, lastly, Wolfgang Streeck has been particularly vocal on this point, arguing that 'democratic capitalism' is determined by 'two conflicting principles . . . of resource allocation': the free deployment of capital in markets

---

2 Steffen Mau, 'Die halbierte Meritokratie', in Steffen Mau and Nadine M. Schöneck, eds, *(Un-)Gerechte (Un-)Gleichheiten*, Berlin, 2015, 38f.

3 A broader overview of this appropriative complex is provided by Torben Iversen, 'Capitalism and Democracy', in Donald A. Wittman and Barry R. Weingast, *The Oxford Handbook of Political Economy*, Oxford and New York, 2006, 601–23.

4 Jürgen Kocka and Wolfgang Merkel, 'Kapitalismus und Demokratie: Kapitalismus ist nicht demokratisch und Demokratie nicht kapitalistisch', in Wolfgang Merkel, ed., *Demokratie und Krise. Zum schwierigen Verhältnis von Theorie und Empirie*, Wiesbaden, 2015, 316.

5 Geoffrey Ingham, *Capitalism*, Cambridge, 2008, 117 and 175.

and redistributive measures 'as certified by the collective choices of democratic politics'.[6] Streeck understands democracy, then, as a regime 'which, in the name of its citizens, deploys public authority to modify the distribution of economic goods resulting from market forces'.[7] Kocka and Merkel likewise invoke the modern 'interventionist welfare state' as a power that exerts a 'regulating, stabilizing and equalizing' influence on market outcomes, so that the actual distribution of wealth needs to be understood as a product of the (usually conflicting) forces of 'democratic institutions and capitalist economics'.[8] The same dualism also runs through Piketty's *Capital in the Twenty-First Century* and Pierre Rosanvallon's *The Society of Equals*.[9]

Readers who are wary of hard and fast social differentiation theories may be sceptical of any sharp analytical distinction between the appropriative complex of the state and the appropriative complex of the markets. However, neither the above-cited authors nor I myself would argue that capitalism and democracy (or rather capitalist markets and the democratic redistributive state) are mutually independent spheres of society. Clearly, markets (if not drug markets) are encouraged,

---

6 Wolfgang Streeck, 'The Crises of Democratic Capitalism', *New Left Review* 71, London, 2011, 7.

7 Streeck, *Buying Time*, 57.

8 Kocka and Merkel, 'Kapitalismus und Demokratie', 317. Needless to say, public policy does not always have an equalizing influence. Stephan Lessenich, for one, has argued that the democratic state is not simply a tool for evening out market disparities, but should be seen as both the architect of these forms of economic distribution and the producer of its own asymmetries (Stephan Lessenich, 'Die Umverteilung nach der Umverteilung: Warum der Kapitalismus den Sozialstaat braucht', in Mau and Schöneck, eds, *(Un-)Gerechte (Un-)Gleichheiten*, 115–24). Nevertheless, it is still the case that the wealthier classes are net contributors and the poorer classes net recipients. In practice, modern Western democracies tend to distribute from the top down.

9 Thomas Piketty, *Capital in the Twenty-First Century*, trans. Arthur Goldhammer, Cambridge, MA, 2014; Pierre Rosanvallon, *The Society of Equals*, trans. Arthur Goldhammer, Cambridge, MA, 2013.

structured and supported by the political establishment, just as the state's capacity to act is dependent on economic value creation processes. Even so, these twin complexes are indeed based on two clearly distinguishable principles or, if you like, two ways of constituting financial solvency. Even if private economic power on one hand and the coercive power of the state on the other, as Geoffrey Ingham puts it, are interdependent,[10] they are nevertheless differently constituted: private economic power (the power to buy or sell – to make payments or cause them to be made) is based on capital ownership (and hence dependent on the rule of law), and therefore – as we saw in Chapter Two – property equals capacity. By contrast, tax-funded redistributive policies – that is, *transfer payments* in the true sense – are made possible not by property rights (or decisions based upon them), but by an intervention in those rights.[11] Transfer payments are made on a compulsory rather than a voluntary basis: they are an imposed obligation. By making tax-funded transfer payments, therefore, the redistributive state is exercising (democratically legitimized) sovereign power.[12] This sovereign capacity, as the cited authors rightly argue, is distinct from the property-based capacity of the capital owner. That does not mean that states are only able to make tax-funded payments. My point is simply that the political economy under discussion here is premised on two different ways of achieving financial solvency: through capital or through sovereign access to capital. Together, these two types of payment have consequences for the pattern of wealth distribution in modern societies that Kocka, Streeck and others

---

10 See Ingham, *Capitalism*, 175.
11 The state is only truly redistributive if it is funded by taxation, and it is strictly in this sense that the term is used here. The tax rates of democratic capitalist societies remain high even in the age of national debt, as anyone who takes a close look at their salary statement will confirm.
12 By contrast, a state that pays its employees with capital borrowed from creditors on the financial markets is engaging in economic practices.

understand as democratic capitalism. The payments resulting from either form of solvency can therefore be said to belong to an appropriative complex which, building on the argument of the above authors, I choose to call the *economic* and the *political* complex. In light of the arguments made in Chapter Three, however, this long-established dualism within capitalism and inequality research now needs to be modified. In reality, most of the distributional effects we are currently witnessing are, to a substantial extent, brought about neither by 'property-based rights of disposal' (economic payments) nor by 'democratic decision-making codes of the political sphere' (political payments),[13] but by keystrokes (para-economic payments). The wealth generated and accumulated via para-economic credit creation can be ascribed neither to the decisions of capital owners nor to the interventions of democratic sovereign powers. The truth is, rather, that wealth is acquired either by voluntary transfer from the previous owner, or by compulsory transfer at the behest of the powers that be, *or* as a result of credit-based money creation. The (unequal) wealth distribution we see today is the result of not just two but three appropriative complexes which generate three different types of income: economic income (arising from decisions regarding property), state transfers (based on democratic sovereignty) and para-economic income (the result of decisions to produce money from scratch). Given how little attention the dualistically oriented studies so far conducted into the origins of material inequality within capitalism have paid to this last element in the wealth triad of *property, sovereign intervention* and *keystrokes*, it is now crucial to subject it to closer scrutiny. How, then, is private wealth created and accumulated within this third appropriative complex or, to put it another way, who are the 'keystroke rentiers'?

---

13 Kocka and Merkel, 'Kapitalismus und Demokratie', 314.

Asset Inflation – the Para-Economic Complex (I)

Keystroke capitalism is characterized by the ability to make investment decisions for the purpose of accumulating capital without having to rely on existing (already accumulated) funds. A second characteristic is the asymmetrical appropriative complex embedding this practice of spontaneous value creation, whereby the return on investment accrues predominantly to those with existing capital. It may be helpful to approach this complex from three angles indicating the different paths of appropriation: firstly, asset inflation (and its consequences); secondly, the integration of banks into corporate complexes; and, last but not least, bank ownership.

To take the first of these, banks generate purchasing power by granting credit (in other words, they buy assets by creating their own liabilities). In advanced economies the world over, private-sector leverage (credit divided by GDP) has been rising for many years.[14] As noted in Chapter One, credit-based purchasing power is growing at a faster rate than the economy. For the purposes of our present inquiry, our first concern should be to establish what the banks originally created all this purchasing power *for* – 'it matters a lot to whom that purchasing power is allocated'.[15] Credit can be granted for new start-ups, to plug shortfalls in state or corporate funding, or to enable the purchase of consumer goods. If you lend someone money to found a company, the founder will spend it on wages, machines and materials. Such investments can promote growth in a positive way because the purchasing power is used to create assets as a means to generate income, from which the loan can then be repaid; in this case, therefore, we can speak of (potentially) 'productive' credit. But credit has

---

14 Adair Turner, *Between Debt and the Devil: Money, Credit, and Fixing Global Finance*, Princeton, 2016, 7.
15 Ibid., 133.

not grown at the same rate as the income measured by GDP, so not all purchasing power can have been generated for productive purposes. Consumer credit can also promote economic growth if it boosts demand, but it risks pushing up the price of consumer goods at the same time. This is what is usually meant when rising or falling inflation is referred to in the media. Despite the vastly increased purchasing power made available by the banks, however, inflation rates among the OECD countries have been falling since the oil crises of the 1970s. Neither economic growth nor consumer price inflation provides much of a clue to the direction of the credit boom. So where did all the extra purchasing power created by the para-economic credit privilege go? Although the trend varies in degree across the advanced economies, it is nevertheless unmistakable: The bulk of bank-generated credit has been used to purchase existing assets. Adair Turner estimates that, since the 1990s, only 15 percent of new loan capital has been created for productive investments in the real economy.[16] Conversely, this means that three quarters of the banks' credit volume – at least until the 2008 crisis – was produced for the purchase and securitization of existing assets. Let us look more closely at the effects of this one-sided use of the para-economic privilege. If credit is granted for a transaction involving existing assets, the price of the assets will (*ceteris paribus*) go up. Buying assets with new credit designed to increase available purchasing power leads to asset price inflation. A major consequence of this process has therefore been to boost the value of

---

16 Ibid.; Adair Turner, 'What Do Banks Do? Why Do Credit Booms and Busts Occur and What Can Public Policy Do About It?', in Adair Turner, Andrew Haldane, Paul Woolley, et al., eds, *The Future of Finance: The LSE Report*, London, 2010, 5–86. The same figure is cited in Joseph Huber, 'Monetäre Modernisierung. Vom Giralgeld zum Vollgeld', in Klaus Kraemer and Sebastian Nessel, eds, *Geld und Krise, Die sozialen Grundlagan moderner Geldordnungen*, Frankfurt am Main, 2015, 296; see also Rana Foroohar, *Makers and Takers: The Rise of Finance and the Fall of American Business*, New York, 2016, 6f.

tradable private assets, which then become more concentrated.[17] Most of the money created for purchasing existing assets during the period in question caused land prices to rise. The lion's share of bank credit in advanced economies generally consists of mortgages. These were not used primarily to finance the construction of new houses, however, but to buy land: some 80 percent of the rise in house prices in the advanced economies between 1950 and 2012 was attributable to the land on which the houses stood.[18] Although real estate ownership is more equitably distributed than creditorship (the ownership of financial assets), this trend has by no means had a levelling effect. For one thing, 'less inequitable' is still pretty inequitable, as real estate too is concentrated among a relatively small number of people, whether in Germany's 'society of renters' or in the home-owning societies of the US or the UK. For another, price rises have assumed extreme proportions, especially in urban centres, while the properties owned by the less well-off are often located in less desirable areas, and are therefore less affected by asset price inflation. In short, not only have high-end properties become disproportionately more expensive, but only the capital-rich can afford to buy them in the first place.[19]

Besides housing, however, the remaining three quarters of the credit volume generated by the financial system was also

---

17   Dirk Bezemer and Michael Hudson, 'Finance Is Not the Economy: Reviving the Conceptual Distinction', *Journal of Economic Issues* 50(3), 2016, 745–68; Turner, *Between Debt and the Devil*; Andrew Jackson and Ben Dyson, *Modernising Money: Why Our Monetary System Is Broken and How It Can Be Fixed*, London, 2014; Huber 'Monetäre Modernisierung'; Foroohar, *Makers and Takers*; European Central Bank, *Annual Report 2016*, available at ecb.europa.eu.

18   Turner, *Between Debt and the Devil*, 67f. On the importance of land to the financialization process, see Jackson and Dyson, *Modernising Money*.

19   Matthew Rognlie, 'Deciphering the Fall and Rise in the Net Capital Share: Accumulation or Scarcity?' in *Brookings Papers on Economic Activity*, 2015.

used to finance derivative-based value chains, which offered major investors average returns of 11 percent in the 1990s and 2000s, causing their wealth to grow much faster than the economy or wages. In the mid-1980s, HNWIs owned assets worth over 7 trillion dollars; in 2000, with the beginning of the boom in derivative securities, that figure was around 25 trillion dollars, and by 2007, it was approximately 41 trillion.[20] These derivative-based value chains benefited moreover from the land boom in that real estate, as 'source collateral', boosted financing volumes outside the regular banking system as well.[21] In this highly complex shadow banking system, the inflation of real estate assets was used to engineer a further inflation of financial returns. This escalation in the price of financial assets is another factor exacerbating inequality. One study of 2015, for example, shows that increases in the value of company shares benefit the richest 5 percent of Europeans at most.[22] It is therefore no accident – as studies of the US show – that wealth inequality correlates with share price development: That is to say, they rise at roughly the same rate.[23]

Asset price inflation is not just a para-economic accumulation of the kind of capital holding that is attractive for purposes of investment or loan security. This steady increase in the value of financial assets is also the force behind the appreciation and depreciation of earned income described in

---

20 Thomas Goda and Photis Lysandrou, 'The Contribution of Wealth Concentration to the Subprime Crisis: A Quantitative Estimation', *Cambridge Journal of Economics* 38(2), 316.

21 Manmohan Singh and Peter Stella, 'Money and Collateral', *IMF Working Paper* 95, 2012.

22 Klaus Adam and Panagiota Tzamourani, 'Distributional Consequences of Asset Price Inflation in the Euro Area', *Discussion Paper der Deutschen Bundesbank* 27, 2015.

23 James K. Galbraith and Travis Hale, 'Income Distribution and the Information Technology Bubble', *University of Texas Inequality Project Working Paper* 27, 2004.

Asset Inflation – the Para-Economic Complex (I)

Chapter One as the dynamo of financialization. In the creation of money from nothing, we have identified a key driver of the value-determining mechanism of financialization. In Chapter One, we noted that the growing importance of financial investments for real-sector companies led to a wage differential, pushing up management salaries and decoupling them from those of the (largely) blue-collar staff who make up the bulk of the workforce. The majority of employees were devalued at the expense of the executive elite. As a result, the left-behind turned to the banks in order to maintain or improve their living standard through private debt (privatized Keynesianism). Because the banks created unlimited new purchasing power with which to buy existing assets, financial investments became increasingly attractive to the non-financial sector, thereby 'reproducing' the demand for credit and leading the banks to create even more new purchasing power. Furthermore, the fact of asset inflation in itself made it increasingly lucrative to borrow in order to acquire sought-after assets and speculate on further price increases, which were (and are) potentially unlimited given the 'hyperelastic' supply of spending power. The upshot was para-economically driven, 'self-reinforcing cycles of credit supply, credit demand, and asset prices', the returns from which accrued to two (more or less overlapping) minorities: the owners of pledgeable and desirable assets and the executive levels of financial and non-financial companies.[24] The deliberate and strategic perpetuation of asset price inflation by some central banks was therefore not just economically but also socially explosive. After the 2008 financial crisis, the Bank of England and the European Central Bank reacted by purchasing huge volumes of assets with a simple keystroke. In short, they did what banks always do: they bought up existing assets with spontaneously created purchasing power. In its 2016 annual report, the European Central Bank notes

---

24   Turner, *Between Debt and the Devil*, 71.

somewhat understatedly: "Wealthier households ... benefited more in relative terms [from this development] compared with poorer households."[25]

Looting Circles – the Para-Economic Complex (II)

There is, however, a second and much more direct way of using asset inflation to generate keystroke returns. One example of this is furnished by electronics giant Apple, which took out a 17-billion-dollar loan in 2013 to buy back its own shares from the market.[26] Such practices are perfectly legal, and nothing unusual. Indeed, in the case of the US there is considerable evidence that they grew in popularity in the wake of financialization. After the 2008 financial crisis, US companies made further cuts to productive investments (such as research and development) and ploughed more money into share buybacks. Through this strategy, businesses are able to inflate their own share price. What makes the Apple example especially noteworthy is that the company was sitting on huge cash reserves at the time: it was evidently cheaper for it to finance the repurchase through borrowing than to use its own liquid funds. Had it drawn on its own cash reserves to buy shares from the market, the volume of available purchasing power would have remained the same. But that is not what happened: instead, a bank created 17 billion dollars' worth of new purchasing power for Apple which the company then used to boost its own value. The man behind this decision was Apple CEO Tim Cook, who is also a major shareholder. In other words, the value of Cook's own portfolio was enhanced with the same keystroke. Indeed, the evidence of the last ten years in particular – at least for the US – indicates that firms have systematically switched to borrowing as a *direct* means of

---

25   European Central Bank, *Annual Report 2016*, 53.
26   Foroohar, *Makers and Takers*.

boosting shareholder value.[27] In this environment, keystroke returns are generated and appropriated based on collaborative relationships. In a modern take on Joseph Schumpeter, the economist James Crotty has pointed out that 'corespective behaviour', meaning cooperative practices from which all parties benefit, is perfectly normal in the supposedly shark-filled waters of capitalism.[28] A capitalist economy is not, after all, a field of perfect competition between unconnected single firms, as the neoclassical economic theory of *homo oeconomicus* would have it. The trouble is that, where banks are concerned, such transactions are not just harmless win-win situations, but arrangements that derive economic advantages from a position of privilege.

Of particular interest here are collaborative value hikes involving members of the same company, or banks that generate purchasing power for their own (part) owners through credit. In order to understand how this kind of thing comes about, and why it is not just a marginal phenomenon, we need to consider two developments. Firstly, banks nowadays tend to belong to groups in which the parent company generally uses credit to co-finance its subsidiaries.[29] Secondly, most banks are not only integrated in banking groups, but are also part of widely ramified corporate networks that (may) cover a variety of business fields. In other words, they belong (partially) to a holding company of some kind, along with many

---

27 For a discussion of this phenomenon in the US, see J.W. Mason, 'Disgorge the Cash: The Disconnect Between Corporate Borrowing and Investment', Roosevelt Institute, 2015; for Europe, the Solactive European Buyback Index has shown the same trend since the beginning of the 2000s.

28 James Crotty, *Capitalism, Macroeconomics and Reality: Understanding Globalization, Financialization, Competition and Crisis*, Cheltenham, UK, 2017.

29 K. J. Martijn Cremers, Rocco Huang and Zacharias Sautner, 'Internal Capital Markets and Corporate Politics in a Banking Group', *The Review of Financial Studies* 24(2), 2011, 358–401; Nicola Cetorelli and Linda Goldberg, 'Liquidity Management of US Global Banks: Internal Capital Markets in the Great Recession', *Federal Reserve Bank of New York Staff Report* 511, 2012.

other companies with whom they can do business. The size and complexity of these structures have grown continuously over the past twenty years or so.[30] What is more, the networks have become denser, so that an ever-increasing share of financial capital is now held by a diminishing number of conglomerates made up of more and more individual firms.[31] The top fifty US financial conglomerates, for example, comprise an average of seventy-six different companies. Both the branches and subsidiaries of the banking groups and the individual firms are often spread over several countries and hence different legal territories. Consequently, different parts of these conglomerates may be subject to totally different regulations and controls. Thanks to the network structure, it is relatively easy within a conglomerate of this kind to generate purchasing power for one's own proprietors. Although sporadic measures were taken after the financial crisis to curb such insider loans (known as 'parental lending') and other forms of circular credit and debt loops, the problem has yet to be tackled comprehensively. This is doubtless due in part to the controversy surrounding the judgement of such practices. In some cases they have been condemned for 'looting the creditors', based on the (incorrect) assumption that bank loans simply distribute saved capital. Indeed, there are instances where that looting has criminal implications. A case in Iceland, for example, was

---

30 Leo Panitch and Sam Gindin, *The Making of Global Capitalism: The Political Economy of American Empire*, London, 2013, 120.

31 In 1990, the top fifty financial groups in the US comprised an average of 5.3 individual subsidiaries. By 1995, there were already 20.2 individual companies per group, rising to 48.7 in 2000 and 63.8 in 2005. By 2010, the average had reached 76.5 (according to my own calculation based on data from Nicola Cetorelli, James McAndrews and James Traina, 'Evolution in Bank Complexity', *Federal Reserve Bank of New York Economic Policy Review* 20(2), 2014, 85–106). For a discussion of the European situation, see Rosa M. Lastra, Rym Ayadi, Rodrigo Olivares-Caminal, et al., 'The Different Legal and Operational Structures of Banking Groups in the Euro Area, and Their Impact on Banks' Resolvability', *Economic and Monetary Affairs Committee In-Depth Analysis*, 2016.

much invoked amid the soul-searching that followed the 2008 financial crisis. Around the turn of the millennium, Iceland had morphed within a few years from a small, largely agrarian state into an internationally renowned financial casino popular with investors. By the early 2000s, the three main banks on the island, which had served the fishing industry right up until the late 1990s, had become major players whose balance sheets boasted financial assets almost ten times the country's economic output. When the turbulence in the global financial system began in 2007, the three big Icelandic banks ran into trouble and ended up going bankrupt. In the aftermath of this catastrophe, it came to light that they had been granting huge amounts of credit to their own holding companies and shareholders.[32] Moreover, large swathes of the banks' shares had been purchased indirectly by the banks themselves, which would issue loans (for instance via their subsidiaries) to an investor who would then use the borrowed capital to buy the shares and deposit them in turn as collateral for the loan. In this way, the banks effectively bought their own shares, whose value had increased in the meantime with every transaction.[33] Although their practices need not necessarily drift into illegality, most banks are, globally speaking, owned by actors who are, at the same time, owners of other companies. In this context, related lending is not uncommon.[34] To anyone working on the assumption that these loans to 'related' companies and entrepreneurs are simply an instance of banks moving assets around, these processes will seem like curious logistical loops. In the case of Iceland, no capital was transferred from its

---

32 Sigridur Benediktsdottir, Jon Danielsson and Gylfi Zoega, 'Lessons from a Collapse of a Financial System', *Economic Policy* 26 (66), 2011, 188.

33 Susan Will, 'The Icelandic Approach to the 2008 Banking Crisis', in Judith van Erp, Wim Huisman, Gudrun Vande Walle, et al., eds, *The Routledge Handbook of White-Collar and Corporate Crime in Europe*, London, 2016.

34 Rafael La Porta, Florencio López-de-Silanes and Guillermo Zamarripa, 'Related Lending', *NBER Working Paper* 8848, 2002.

owner to their bank and back again: Instead, capital was created for the owner of the bank. The privilege of producing purchasing power generates returns which can thus be appropriated directly by bank owners. What we are talking about here, then, is emphatically not (in most cases) the looting of savings, but the looting of a para-economic privilege. As such, these recursive relationships between companies and their proprietors can be confidently described as 'looting circles'.[35] There is substantial evidence to suggest that these circles are not the exception, but rather the rule of the financialized global economy. It is only in recent years that social scientists have begun to notice how much of a crossover there really is between ownership and the concentration of corporate capital. Central to this discovery are the studies by Glattfelder, Vitali and Battiston.[36] Via an elaborate network analysis, these researchers studied the ownership structure of transnational corporations in order to determine the true extent of mutual overlap – that is, how dense the network of capital control is. They came to the astonishing conclusion that the global economy is sustained by a 'backbone' of just 147 companies which are, to all intents and purposes, mutually affiliated. In fact, the degree of overlap is so great that the authors of the study refer – somewhat controversially but not without justification – to a single 'super-entity'. According to the study, this quasi-corporation controls 40 percent of transnational capital assets. A slightly larger chunk of the network with a slightly lower concentration of 'ownership ties' (737 firms) controls 80 percent.[37]

---

35 Aaron Sahr, 'Reichtum aus Feenstaub: Das Free-Lunch-Privileg des Keystroke-Kapitalismus', in Heinz Bude and Philipp Staab, eds, *Kapitalismus und Ungleichheit. Die neuen Verwerfungen*, Frankfurt/New York, 2016, 25–44.

36 Stefania Vitali, James B. Glattfelder and Stefano Battiston, 'The Network of Global Corporate Control', ArXiv Reprint, 28 July 2011, available at arXiv.org; James B. Glattfelder, *Decoding Complexity: Uncovering Patterns in Economic Networks*, Heidelberg, 2013.

37 Vitali et al., 'The Network of Global Corporate Control', 6.

Although the detailed calculations of this study have also attracted some criticism,[38] the general trend is indisputable: More and more assets are becoming concentrated within a few large holding networks with overlapping owners. In other words, the growth of financial assets and financial returns we have seen for decades has taken place within networks consisting of a small number of proprietors, which means that, even though payment promises are in many cases still made between formally independent firms, in practice, they are highly likely to involve the production of assets for a customer with fingers in both pies. Statistically, therefore, one would expect looting circles to be more common than might appear at first sight. That such studies lend plausibility to the argument, rather than simply stating in numbers how much purchasing power is generated for internal and how much for external proprietors, testifies to a lack of available data. To date, there has never been a systematic examination of these circles (either by private or administrative authorities). Generally speaking, company-internal payments – and hence also the internal generation of keystroke purchasing power – are not particularly well documented or represented by the available statistics.[39] This urgently needs to change if we are to have a transparent debate about the legitimacy of such processes. To be blunt, not until we have better data on looting circles can we hope to improve the stability of the global financial system and bring about a proper evaluation and democratic discussion of the relationship between keystroke returns and inequality.

---

38 A good overview of the early debate, primarily in blog form, can be found at: http://j-node.blogspot.de/2011/08/network-of-global-corporate-control.html.

39 Cremers et al., 'Internal Capital Markets', 1.

Interest Income – the Para-Economic Complex (III)

A third means of appropriating para-economic returns is to own a company with a banking licence – not just because the bank can create new purchasing power for the owners within an ownership network, but also for the much more obvious reason that banks are lucrative businesses. After the 2008 financial crisis, Bertolt Brecht's proverbial advice that it is better to found a bank than to rob one was on everybody's lips. Indeed, the banking system of the wealthy OECD countries has boomed since the abandonment of the gold standard at the 1973 Bretton Woods conference, and quite spectacularly so in the wake of the self-reinforcing financialization process: After remaining stable at roughly 10 to 12 percent between 1948 and 1980, the financial share of the US economy's total annual profits rose to 30 percent in 2007. The continuous expansion of the money supply due to para-economic lending meant that hefty profits were made from fees and interest charges and distributed to bank owners in the form of dividends. Recently, ownership of the world's 1,000 biggest banks brought in annualized pre-tax returns of around 15 percent.[40] The banks' profitability is partly attributable, as we have seen, to the establishment of a cyclical dynamic of asset price inflation followed by a corresponding rise in demand for bank credit, but the negligible production costs of purchasing power also play their part. To quote Jeremy Rifkin, 'keystroke' money is effectively a 'zero marginal cost product'.[41] And, here, we come up against the wider question of what to make of the whole practice of earning money – broadly speaking, interest income – from lending based on the para-economic privilege.

---

40 Andrew Haldane, Simon Brennan and Vasileios Madouros, 'What Is the Contribution of the Financial Sector: Miracle or Mirage?' in Adair Turner, Andrew Haldane, Paul Woolley, et al., eds, *The Future of Finance, The LSE Report*, London, 2010, 90.

41 Jeremy Rifkin, *The Zero Marginal Cost Society*, New York, 2014.

A sensitive topic, to be sure, but a necessary one if we are to offer a general assessment of this third appropriative complex.

One can argue that banks receive fees and interest payments in return for producing purchasing power. Suspicion of businesspeople who make their money from loan interest can be found throughout history from Ancient Greece through medieval Christianity to the Arab Islamic world. Aristotle famously relegated moneymaking to the lowlier science of chrematistics, setting it apart from the approved art of household management, which basically revolved around arable farming. (In his evaluation of its merits, Aristotle did not bother to consider that farming, unlike moneylending, relied on enslaved labour.) Both the Christian Church and the Islamic faith condemned interest as an 'unnatural' accumulation of capital that was not meant to be accumulated. God (to stick with the Western version) had given man the earth so that he could till the soil and extract its fruits. Anyone who, having earned their money from 'honest' toil, went on to lend it in order to profit over and over again from God's gifts in the form of interest and, even more controversially, compound interest, was a sinner. Such scruples no longer encumber the modern global economy and its accompanying science of economics, in which interest is considered an unproblematic and necessary component of capitalism. Even in the Middle Ages, when the Church was most vehement in its condemnation, the practice of charging interest was routine: People simply invented various tricks to avoid calling it by name. But here's the point: Modern economic theory justifies interest payments with the liberal argument of the right to free enjoyment of property. The influential economist Paul Samuelson, for example, states: 'Interest rates or returns on investments are the price of borrowing or lending money.'[42] This makes perfect sense if we assume – as

---

42 Paul Samuelson and William Nordhaus, *Economics*, London, 1948, 284.

economic textbooks generally do – that credit is contingent upon accumulated ownership: that is, it relies on savings being available for borrowing. Viewed thus, interest payments – as any scholar of classical banking theory will tell you – are premiums charged by investors who not only forgo the possibility of doing anything else with their capital for the term of the loan (liquidity premium) but also assume a risk in the process (risk premium).[43] Thus, interest should be understood in relation to these two types of costs. The trouble is that neither of these observations correspond to reality (or at least no longer entirely). Credit is not generated by transferring capital taken from someone else; therefore interest cannot be a liquidity premium since no one is temporarily forfeiting their liquidity. Consequently, no 'costs' are due by way of compensation for the inability to access one's property for the period in question. A borrower does not 'use' another person's money, but instead borrows money specifically created for the purpose, and which would not have existed but for the need to borrow it. For this reason, authors such as Ann Pettifor, L. Randall Wray and Steven Keen argue persistently that our present monetary system is dependent on borrowers in order to generate purchasing power – and hence economic activity – in the first place.[44] Counterintuitive though it may sound, without debts – and indeed, without people willing to get into debt – there would be no 'circulatable liabilities'. That is, there would be no money.

It is certainly true that banks take a risk by granting credit: after all, having once created the money, they then have to

---

43 On the classical banking and credit theory still dominant within economics, see Aaron Sahr, *Das Versprechen des Geldes. Eine Praxistheorie des Kredits*, Hamburg, 2017, 160–86.

44 Ann Pettifor, *The Production of Money: How to Break the Powers of Bankers*, London, 2017; L. Randall Wray, *Modern Money Theory: A Primer on Macroeconomics for Sovereign Money Systems*, New York, 2012; Steve Keen, *Debunking Economics: The Naked Emperor Dethroned*, London, 2011.

'uncreate' it. Normally, the sum brought into existence by the extension of a loan (regardless of capital reserves) disappears again when the loan is paid off. If the debt is not repaid, however, the bank has to draw on its own funds for this purpose. Fortunately for banks, these risks are spread over many shoulders, thanks to the extensive subsidization mechanisms established by capitalist democracies after World War II. For one thing, central banks can be relied upon as lenders of last resort who, in exceptional circumstances, will even go as far as to erase bad debts from private banks' accounts and provide fresh capital in exchange. For another, the state guarantees retail banking through deposit insurance, thereby shielding private banks from the pressures of the market. Furthermore, the lasting impact of the Great Depression has led capitalist countries to respond to the numerous financial crises since 1945 with systematic countermeasures, so that the financial sector no longer has to bear the day-to-day burden of its self-generated credit risks all by itself – a form of implicit subsidy, as explained in Chapter One.[45] In short, moneylending fees and interest payments that generate profits for private companies cannot be regarded either as a liquidity premium for creditors, or entirely as a risk premium. Therefore, we need a new narrative for interest, which might look something like this: As private service providers, banks supply a good essential to the economy as a whole, namely money or purchasing power – the medium necessary in order to access scarce resources, initiate value creation processes and satisfy needs. As a universal means of exchange, money can also be defined as part of the infrastructure, not very different from, say, the public good of legal certainty. It is, as Joseph Huber expresses it, a 'circulating common good that is constantly changing

---

45 Moritz Schularick and Alan Taylor, 'Credit Booms Gone Bust: Monetary Policy, Leverage Cycles and Financial Crises, 1870–2008', *NBER Working Paper* 15512, 2009, 4.

hands'.[46] Both legal certainty and money are needed by all economic actors in order to be able to function reliably as goods. Legal certainty is provided by the state as a public good, while money creation is privatized. This being the case, it is reasonable to ask who bears the costs of, and who reaps the benefits from, this privatization of a circulating common good. Many public goods formerly provided by the state are now produced by private-sector companies – from energy, postal and telecommunication systems to EU border security. The privatizers' argument is always the same: Markets can offer post and telecoms services much more cheaply than the bureaucratic apparatus of the state ever could – and it is true that telephone costs are much lower today than they were before privatization. But how can the same argument be advanced for the privatization of money creation when its production costs are zero? As history shows, there is no lack of alternatives to this arrangement. For a long time, the profit made from issuing currency, known as seigniorage, provided political rulers with their third largest income source after tax revenue and debt. Nowadays, by contrast, we have become accustomed to a privatized system of seigniorage: The proceeds from money creation accrue predominantly to private companies, with only a very small proportion going (via central bank profit) to the state. What is more, governments today actually subsidize this revenue, thereby supporting the process that allows consumption levels to be sustained increasingly by private debt. Such a policy keeps demand high and ensures a constant supply of private seigniorage for bank managers and proprietors – and hence also for managers of financialized companies and owners of attractive capital assets.

This unequal division of labour between money-generating banks and security-providing states also has socio-structural consequences. The costs of privatized money creation are borne

---

46 Huber, 'Monetäre Modernisierung', 302.

by the middle and lower classes: They are net interest payers while asset holders are net interest recipients.[47]

In conclusion, it is fair to say that the general public (as a political community) and the middle and lower classes (as socio-structural groups) bear the costs of para-economic money creation, while private companies and the wealthy retain the profits. The interest paid by the poorer majority to the richer minority is not a gratuity in return for the favour of lending their property, but rather a charge for the exercise of a privilege, a 'rent' in the classical sense of the word – an extra- or para-economic income based on a position of dominance rather than a service of any kind.[48] In this sense, the credit system is a bottom-up redistributive mechanism, an appropriative complex that turns the decision makers of the banks, their owners and – via the mechanisms of asset price inflation – top earners and the wealthy into the rentiers of keystroke capitalism.

#change

In making this case, we should not gloss over the impossibility of accurately quantifying the contribution of para-economic purchasing power to the inequality crisis. Disappointing though this is, it partly reflects the conceptual flaws – already inherent in the data we have available to make sense of the economy, both as scientists and as a democratic community– of a school of thought that only recognizes capitalist and non-capitalist economies, and no para-economic forms of

---

47 Graham Hodgson, 'Banking, Finance and Income Inequality', Positive Money, October 2013, available at positivemoney.org; see also Jackson and Dyson, *Modernising Money*, 156.

48 See Bruno S. Frey, 'Märkte, Gerechtigkeit und die Rolle von Vielfalt', in Steffen Mau and Nadine M. Schöneck, eds, *(Un-)Gerechte (Un-)Gleichheiten*, Berlin, 2015, 85; Bezemer and Hudson, 'Finance Is Not the Economy'.

capitalism. Even the most sceptical reader, however, would find it hard to downplay the dynamic impact of financialization on the economy as a whole in terms of the attractiveness of financial capital, bank ownership and the assumption of management roles within corporate structures. This process is rendering the entire economy increasingly reliant on the unlimited supply of credit willingly (and profitably) dispensed by banks. It is no coincidence that, during the period from 1970 to 2010, private banks increased the available purchasing power in the wealthy OECD economies by a factor of around seventy-seven.[49] The inequality crisis cannot be explained without reference to the driving force of para-economic credit, and with it the para-economic appropriative complex.

If a discussion panel were to be asked whether and on what basis they thought it reasonable to criticize Walter White, Jesse Pinkman and their drug cartel collaborators for appropriating the profits from methamphetamine production, they would no doubt reach a broad consensus. Crystal meth is an illegal drug, and the profits from these value creation processes are therefore likewise illegal. Not to mention that the financial exploitation of addicts is undoubtedly morally questionable – although even that normative judgement can no longer be considered universal (at least, it hardly seems to bother anyone in the case of alcohol). The practice by which (a few) entrepreneurs and wealthy individuals are able to profit from the para-economic privilege of banks is, in the vast majority of cases, legal; any wider discussion of the rights and wrongs of such legal income (and the resulting wealth distribution) will therefore invoke the concept of justice. From a sociological perspective, this is dodgy territory. Moralizations are, rightly enough, not sociology's style, and notions of justice are so culturally diverse and vague in terms of actual empirical beliefs that a constructive analysis becomes problematic.

---

49 Sahr, *Das Versprechen des Geldes*, 14.

Nonetheless, there is one thing we should be clear about: As far as I can see, none of the prevailing theories legitimizing income and wealth disparities appear to offer any source of legitimization for para-economic revenue. Paradoxical as it may sound, radical proponents of the paradigm of individual freedom – often referred to disparagingly as 'economic liberals' or 'neoliberals' – cannot defend the keystroke rentiers with their usual arguments. In light of this observation, the next and final chapter of this book will attempt to explore the possible avenues for reforming keystroke capitalism.

V
Change

The development of capitalist economies in the US and Europe has been characterized since the late 1970s by three notable features: Firstly, the volume of private wealth has reached a new high virtually year on year; secondly, we have seen consistently record-breaking levels of private debt; and thirdly, both wealth and debt have become more unevenly distributed than ever. The trend towards greater equality has gone into reverse. This inequality crisis is attributable to a range of factors, a few of which I have highlighted in this book: namely the financialization process and with it the rise of the para-economic value creation system and the corresponding appropriative complex of 'keystroke capitalism'. The reason for my emphasis on this point is not that financialization depresses wages due to the expansion of international competition brought about by globalization, or that everything can be put down to structural assumptions about capital returns in periods of declining economic growth. Rather, my aim has been to assemble evidence of the relevance to the inequality crisis of a source of wealth that financialization has brought to the fore. That source of wealth (or type of payment) is conspicuously absent from the prevailing view of capitalism as synonymous with 'capitalist economics', in the sense of an interface between capital ownership and labour ownership. Not all variants of capitalism as a social practice can be understood in terms of ownership, or the power to act that is conferred by already existing assets. In modern societies, capital gains come from three sources: economic payments by capital owners, political payments by ruling authorities, and para-economic payments by privileged actors, namely banks, which create purchasing power and debt in lockstep, irrespective of pre-accumulated capital reserves. For the most part, therefore, the huge disparities in wealth are not just attributable to economic inequalities engendered by exchange markets (trading places for scarce goods facilitated and structured by the right of ownership) in which the redistributive state intervenes as a (largely) equalizing force by issuing payment orders; they also proceed from distributional effects of the banks' ability to create purchasing power via 'keystroke' credit. Although the impact of these three appropriative complexes (basically markets, states and credit), each of which arise from a different kind of 'power',[1] cannot be precisely quantified, it is nevertheless perfectly possible to make qualified statements about observable trends. As the lending and borrowing curve has become progressively decoupled from economic output since around 1980, so the influence of the para-economic complex has increased relative to the economic one. While the tax rate is comparatively stable in many OECD countries, top tax rates and corporation taxes have been widely reduced and social security contributions rolled back in the wake of the 'neoliberal revolution'.[2] The levelling effect exerted by the appropriative complex of the redistributive state has diminished in recent decades; this erosion of the 'social rights of citizenship' in advanced OECD societies is a process well documented in sociology.[3] Furthermore, the fact that the welfare state is increasingly funded by borrowing has made it a reliable source of credit demand over

---

[1] Ann Pettifor, for example, refers to 'credit power' in this context in *The Production of Money: How to Break the Powers of Bankers*, London, 2017.

[2] Wolfgang Streeck, *Buying Time*, trans. Patrick Camiller and David Fernbach, London, 2017.

[3] Ibid., 45; see also Oliver Nachtwey, *Germany's Hidden Crisis: Social Decline in the Heart of Europe*, trans. David Fernbach and Loren Balhorn, London/New York, 2018; Pierre Rosanvallon, *The Society of Equals*, trans. Arthur Goldhammer, Cambridge, MA, 2013.

the past decades, thereby feeding the para-economic appropriative complex with its bottom-up redistribution mechanism. *The inequality crisis is a consequence of the constellation of an asymmetrical economic appropriative complex, a weakened political one and a flourishing para-economic one.* This is an insight that no contemporary social debate on capitalism and inequality can afford to ignore.[4] To be properly considered, however, it needs to be freed from the all too rigid frame of reference that exists between the opposite poles of the free market and a strong welfare state. The analysis, evaluation and, where appropriate, critique of keystroke capitalism should not be framed as a choice between freedom of economic activity and the solidarity aspirations of democratic communities, or, as Niklas Luhmann puts it, a choice between 'random' distribution of wealth via the markets or a 'communistic' distribution via the state.[5] The real question is who is entitled to the privilege of creating money from nothing, or who can be reasonably entrusted with it. Para-economic money creation undermines traditional debating structures and justification models, and this alone gives it a legitimatory homelessness, which I shall take as a starting point in my conclusion to reflect on possible change.

---

4 While the relevance of keystroke capitalism to rising inequality within the advanced economies can hardly be disputed, one caveat is nevertheless in order. The wealth pyramid takes into account households and household assets. This paints a misleading picture in that households are not homogeneous empirical entities that are openly identifiable within the social reality. If we were to break households down by gender, ethnicity or age, we would get a very different impression of the inequality crisis (and a differently shaped pyramid). While it would be absurd to downplay the impact of such social distinctions, my focus lies – with good reason – elsewhere: gender, ethnicity and age inequalities operate within the three appropriative complexes. Women and ethnic minorities are treated less favourably on the labour market by investors, and they do not have the same borrowing opportunities as '(old) white men'. Disparities in income and wealth distribution due to social factors are likewise the result of economic, para-economic or sovereign payment transactions and thus stem from the same appropriative triad.

5 Niklas Luhmann, *Rechtssystem und Rechtsdogmatik*, Stuttgart, 1974.

Legitimatory Homelessness

People do not generally take to the streets to protest the fact that no two individuals are the same size; they do so, rather, to denounce discrimination on the basis of gender or ethnicity or call out the injustice of wealth distribution systems and persuade those they hold responsible to take action. Unlike natural differences, social inequalities are deemed to require legitimation. That does not mean that they have to be explained or justified with reference to higher, more abstract ideals through philosophical or sociological discourse. Accordingly, it cannot be the task of sociology to pronounce on the *legitimacy* of social orders, processes or circumstances; rather, its focus should be on the *processes* of legitimation, that is, how society arrives at justification models that are more or less universally accepted. In this context, sociology has three functions: firstly, it can and should investigate empirically which theories and arguments are actually deployed – that is, in social practice – in relation to the legitimacy or illegitimacy of social orders, processes or circumstances. Its second concern is to identify which power constellations allow particular justification models to become established as more or less hegemonic social legitimation discourses, and with what social consequences. Thirdly and finally – and herein lies the sum and substance of this concluding chapter – sociological studies can attempt to highlight problem configurations, imbalances or nodes with the aim of stimulating social debate on the legitimacy of social arrangements. Such studies probably belong to the strand of the discipline known as 'public sociology'.[6] My aim here, then, is not to act as a critic or defender of keystroke

---

6 Michael Burawoy, 'For Public Sociology', *Soziale Welt* 56(4), 2005, 347–74; Heinz Bude, 'Auf der Suche nach einer öffentlichen Soziologie', *Soziale Welt* 56(4), 2005, 375–80.

rentiers myself but to demonstrate, in the interest of breaking down entrenched self-conceptions, that there is nothing among all the sophistry used by society to justify income and wealth disparities that legitimizes their special status. Models that attempt to rationalize asymmetries in wealth distribution with the customary notions of *justice*, for example, are confounded by the effects of a para-economic appropriative complex strengthened by financialization. To put it bluntly, even passionate neoliberals who champion unregulated markets and fly the flag of libertarianism would have to concede the legitimatory homelessness of keystroke capitalism. Criticism of the money creation privilege is therefore not automatically the preserve of the political left, but could be voiced with equal vehemence by the liberal centre. In the interest of focusing more closely on that privilege, I am drawing here on a necessarily selective and condensed account of basic patterns, but one that ought nevertheless to be informative.[7]

When it comes to differentiating between just and unjust wealth and income, we can, on one hand, set the bar deliberately high and call for *needs-based justice*. This means that income and wealth are justified to the extent necessary to satisfy our needs (howsoever defined), such as a basic level of accommodation, food and so on. By this measure, however, any wealth over and above those needs would be either unjust per se or irrelevant to the justice debate and better judged by other criteria. It is surely indisputable that the nigh-on 117 trillion dollars of private wealth belonging to the richest 0.7 percent of the world's population cannot be justified on the basis that the 0.7 percent *need* the same amount as the remaining 99.3 percent who own roughly the other half of

---

7 My remarks here are based very broadly on Gert G. Wagner, 'Ungleichheit muss nicht ungerecht sein – sie ist aber oft unvernünftig', in Steffen Mau and Nadine M. Schöneck, eds, *(Un-)Gerechte (Un-)Gleichheiten*, Berlin, 2015, 46–53.

global wealth.[8] Any attempt to adapt keystroke capitalism to empirical reality is doomed from the start, however, by the trivial fact that the revenue from money creation results from a privilege and, as in the case of asset inflation, is completely divorced from need.

A second commonly applied principle for distinguishing between just and unjust wealth (or its distribution) is that of *equality of opportunity*. According to this line of argument, the appropriation of wealth is justified if it takes place via accessible and transparent distributive mechanisms allowing all parties to participate on an equal footing. These mechanisms are generally considered to be embodied by (idealized) markets where goods (including labour) are exchanged. Many people intuitively accept the principle of equal opportunity, and numerous government measures such as educational support are justified on this basis. Far fewer, however, would defend the claim that the current distribution of income and wealth is the result of an already level playing field that effectively legitimizes the status quo. At least, such a paradigm cannot be reasonably argued in the case of para-economic value creation processes. True, large numbers of people have the opportunity to borrow, but only on widely different terms. Those with the highest credit ratings are those in possession of assets which they can offer as security.[9] Furthermore, the para-economic appropriative complex directs the keystroke

---

[8] Credit Suisse, *Global Wealth Databook 2016*, Zurich, 2016. Criticizing capitalist economies on the basis of equal need is, moreover, often fruitless, since there is no generally accepted scale for measuring need. It might be possible to agree on the legitimacy of a given articulated need relative to a universal minimum, although that would only account for a fraction of economic value creation. Any attempt to measure the distribution of, say, iPhones or penthouse flats based purely on the abstract criterion of equality of need is, however, doomed to failure. Such critiques are therefore generally directed less at the markets than at the state as a provider of basic social security.

[9] Geoffrey Ingham refers to a Matthew effect in *The Nature of Money*, Cambridge, 2004, 138.

returns to a minority of individuals who are already wealthy and/or in managerial positions. By contrast, the opportunities of wage-dependent blue-collar workers to accumulate capital by saving and hence to become rentiers themselves have been steadily eroded by financialization.

A third principle advanced to justify economic disparities is the meritocratic principle, otherwise known as *performance-based justice*. From this perspective, income and wealth are legitimately earned if they reflect the service performed or promised by their owner. Once again, this principle is generally applied to the market as a distributive mechanism. Some market economy theorists – and, as we know from the press and research, many capitalist actors – have credited the free market with the ability to dispense precisely this kind of justice.[10] According to these theorists, those who earn a high income on the market or obtain a particularly high price for a product can only do so if their performance warrants it. Otherwise the market would simply reward a higher-performing supplier offering their service or product at a lower price. This argument has been deployed particularly forcefully in the debate over management salaries and bonuses for top earners. In 2012, for example, there was much debate in Germany over the 17-million-euro pay cheque of Volkswagen boss Martin Winterkorn, which, it was claimed in the media, was around 400 times the wages of a skilled worker within the same corporation.[11] The studies by Sighard Neckel and others cited in Chapter One on the decoupling of management salaries from general market principles cast doubt on the empirical relevance of the meritocratic principle. And even if one were to persist, without any empirical basis, in the belief that market-generated earned income is commensurate with the earner's

---

10 Sighard Neckel, 'Die Ungleichheit der Märkte', in Mau and Schöneck, eds, *(Un-)Gerechte (Un-)Gleichheiten*, 93–103.

11 Julian Bank, 'Mr Winterkorn's Pay: A Typology of Justification Patterns of Income Inequality', *Social Justice Research* 29(2), 228–52.

performance, long-term historical reality would still bear out the trend highlighted by Piketty – that markets usually reward capital input more generously than labour input. Accordingly, even the claim that the original purpose of wealth was to reward performance could hardly justify a situation where past rewards can be continually redeployed in order to accumulate more and more wealth. The assumption that free market prices reward a level of performance identifiable without regard to those prices is empirically false. This observation does no damage to normative concepts (perhaps it even benefits them), but it does make the inequality crisis and keystroke capitalism less likely to be legitimized and approved on the basis of performance-based justice. Whichever way you look at it, the fact remains that asset inflation rewards ownership (and hence, at best, past performance), and interest earnings reward privilege.

To pursue this justification model any further, we would have to equate performance with the achieved market price. In that case, we would be forced to argue that the mere fact that A earns more on the market than B proves the difference in their performance. Technically, however, we would then be encroaching on another justificatory argument, as demonstrated by Gert G. Wagner, for example. Wagner explains the failure of the meritocratic justification strategy by arguing that differences in performance are not measurable or comparable, just as the sporting achievements of weight lifters and pole vaulters cannot be ranked hierarchically on the basis of performance. Consequently, the question of why a successful investment banker earns more than a care worker can only be answered as follows: 'Because the bank earns more than the care home ... This disparity in pay has nothing to do with individual effort. Ultimately, the economic performance of a business ... depends entirely on the demand for its products or services.'[12] However,

---

12 Wagner, 'Ungleichheit muss nicht ungerecht sein', 49.

by identifying performance with the customer's willingness to pay, we are no longer using an external criterion – that of performance – to legitimize income, but in effect declaring the income earned on the market intrinsically just. Therefore, Wagner argues, economic performance is essentially measured by nothing more than 'the price obtained for an economic good or service'.[13] Strictly speaking, however, this draws on the argument of those who attempt to justify income and wealth disparities, which stems from classical liberalism.[14] Authors such as John Locke, Friedrich von Hayek, Milton Friedman and Robert Nozick have deployed a 'historical' argument to legitimize income and wealth in free constitutional states that still persists in contemporary liberal discourse. This argument considers any income just that is obtained under just conditions. From a liberal perspective, however, 'just' conditions are achieved not by distributing wealth according to need, performance or equality of opportunity, but by guaranteeing the freedom of the individual through rights – and in the context of capital assets, rights to private ownership. For ownership rights to be fully asserted and protected, the owner must be able to transfer their property freely. Hence, a just use of one's wealth to make a purchase results, thanks to 'the formal justice of the market', in a legitimate capital gain for the seller.[15] The disparity in income between the banker and the carer is just if the bank's customers, by disposing freely of their money, voluntarily made payments of an order of magnitude that gave rise to that income. For this reason, Friedrich Hayek famously declared the concept of social justice a failure.[16] In his view, it is impermissible for a society of free individuals to place further demands on the

---

13 Ibid., 50.
14 For an overview, see Wolfgang Kersting, *Theorien der sozialen Gerechtigkeit*, Stuttgart, 2000.
15 Streeck, *Buying Time*, 61.
16 Friedrich August von Hayek, *Law, Legislation and Liberty, Volume 2: The Mirage of Social Justice*, Chicago, 1976.

distributional situations resulting from freely made decisions. As Milton Friedman also argues, intervening in the outcomes of free buying and selling decisions is tantamount to restricting ownership rights in the first place.[17] In a free society, according to the liberal social philosopher Nozick, people acquire property (leaving aside its 'original' appropriation) via 'just transfers' from the previous owner: 'A person who acquires a holding in accordance with the principle of justice in transfer, from someone else entitled to the holding, is entitled to the holding.'[18] In other words, as long as property is transferred on a voluntary basis, the resulting increase in wealth is legitimate.

Liberal economic justifications of material inequality like Wagner's are often obliged to fall back on this classic defence of asset acquisition. But classical liberalism, with its principle of 'justice as exchange', offers an argumentation model that only works for income derived from payments that are based on ownership rights.[19] It applies exclusively to the wealth effects of practices allowing the disposition of scarce resources by the holder of such rights. In other words, even this rudimentary liberal justification model for wealth accumulation is torpedoed by the money creation privilege of the banks. We are not talking here about asset transfers that depend on the freedom of private ownership, but about payments arising from nowhere. In actual fact, therefore, the act of scrutinizing the beneficiaries of this privilege has nothing to do with allowing one's view to be coloured by politics – you do not need to have anti-liberal views to venture a critical look at those who profit from keystroke value creation. If anything, economically liberal parties ought to be firmly on board with this endeavour if they are truly liberal rather than simply paying lip service

---

17 Milton Friedman, *Capitalism and Freedom*, 40th anniversary ed., Chicago, 2002, 7–21 and 161–76.
18 Robert Nozick, *Anarchy, State and Utopia*, New York, 1974, 151.
19 Otfried Höffe, *Political Justice: Foundations For a Critical Philosophy of Law and the State*, trans. Jeffrey C. Cohen, Cambridge, 1995.

to the concept. To attempt to justify keystroke capitalism under the guise of liberalism is merely to defend the privileges of wealth.

Unstable and Dysfunctional

Those who are loath to mess with the fluid concept of justice may attempt to construct a functionalist legitimation of keystroke capitalism. Social arrangements can, as we know, be 'unjust but useful'.[20] But, even here, evidence of the legitimatory homelessness of this specific practice and its appropriative effects is mounting. The economic dysfunctionality of unlimited private money creation is already implicit in the arguments of the previous chapters; since it has been examined in much greater detail by other commentators, however, a mere mention of the problems will suffice here.[21] In short, everything that is wrong with this model can be encapsulated in the concept of *procyclicality*. At present, new money is created whenever a potential borrower succeeds in convincing a bank that he can and will repay the debt. Or, to put it another way, whenever a bank deems a customer creditworthy, purchasing power is generated. Because the banks' credit supply is 'hyperelastic',

---

20 André Kieserling, 'Ungerecht, aber nützlich. Zur Verteilung der wissenschaftlichen Reputation', in Mau and Schöneck, eds, *(Un-)Gerechte (Un-)Gleichheiten*, 54–62.

21 Josh Ryan-Collins, Tony Greenham, Richard Werner, et al., *Where Does Money Come From? A Guide to the UK Monetary and Banking System*, London, 2011; Andrew Jackson and Ben Dyson, *Modernising Money: Why Our Monetary System Is Broken and How It Can Be Fixed*, London, 2014; Mary Mellor, *Debt or Democracy. Public Money for Sustainability and Social Justice*, London, 2016; Joseph Huber, 'Monetäre Modernisierung. Vom Giralgeld zum Vollgeld', in Klaus Kraemer and Sebastian Nessel, eds, *Geld und Krise, Die sozialen Grundlagan moderner Geldordnungen*, Frankfurt am Main, 2015, 291–308; Adair Turner, *Between Debt and the Devil: Money, Credit, and Fixing Global Finance*, Princeton, 2016; Pettifor, *The Production of Money*; Aaron Sahr, *Das Versprechen des Geldes. Eine Praxistheorie des Kredits*, Hamburg, 2017.

meaning it can respond to any demand the banks judge to be profitable, there is no limit to the formation of speculative bubbles in times of economic expansion. The early 2000s, prior to the financial crisis of 2008, offer a prime example of how more and more loan applications for increasingly risky investments and debt-intensive financing and business models were approved, thereby triggering the creation of new purchasing power.[22] In times of economic boom, more and more creditors think they can go on perpetually incurring and repaying debts. This is fine for a while, because the constant supply of borrowers and debt ensures the production of the currency needed to pay off existing loans. But such booms also create a problem. Purchasing power is generated when people incur debts; when they repay them, the supply is accordingly reduced. If the optimism of creditors and debtors begins to wane again at some point, prompting a fall in the demand for new debt (and hence in the production of purchasing power), or indeed the clearance of old debt, this can rapidly lead to a climate of growing doubt about whether the debts that have accumulated in tandem with monetary assets can be repaid. This was the case in 2007 and 2008, although numerous credit crises of a similar nature had already occurred in the previous decades.[23] It is no coincidence that the global figures published by the International Monetary Fund for the period between 1970 and 2007 record 124 crises involving entire banking systems (not just individual institutes), 326 currency crises and 64 public debt crises.[24] This equates to an average of almost fourteen financial crises per year. Another problem associated

---

22 For references and findings, see Sahr, *Das Versprechen des Geldes*, 231–92.

23 Mellor, *Debt or Democracy*, 27.

24 Luc Laeven and Fabián Valencia, 'Systematic Banking Crises Database: An Update', *IMF Working Paper* 163, 2012; see also Huber, 'Monetäre Modernisierung'; Carmen Reinhart and Kenneth Rogoff, *This Time Is Different: Eight Centuries of Financial Folly*, Princeton, 2011.

with the boom and bust mechanism of keystroke capitalism is that credit does not necessarily produce money for productive purposes; consequently, the expansion of the money supply in boom times (at least over the past forty years) may have inflated asset prices, but it has done nowhere near as much to sustain the economic value creation processes capable of generating the income needed for debt repayments in boom or bust. Keystroke capitalism increases capital (and hence debt) during economic upturns, but reduces it abruptly at times of crisis, because the money supply is only stable as long as there is a steady stream of new borrowers to make up for its diminution by repaying outstanding loans. As a result, when the economy takes a dive, there is a shortage of investment capital but the debt mountain remains. 'Procyclicality', in short, means that private bank lending amplifies trends without applying any effective moderating or compensatory mechanisms, so that credit mushrooms in the boom phase and becomes scarce in the bust phase. In this way, para-economic value creation by banks not only creates inequality, but also leads to economic instability and actually prevents capital from being directed to socially necessary projects.

While the absence of functional legitimation models in itself does nothing to change the existing social arrangements, sociology can nevertheless endeavour to open up social debates and throw light on alternative ways of thinking by pointing to the 'legitimacy deficit of "keystroke capitalism"'.[25] Financial system reforms implemented since the 2008 crisis show positive and important first steps towards extending conventional control principles, but ignore the money creation privilege itself. Similarly, voices in the debate over how to solve the inequality crisis fail – with the exception of those cited here – to drill down to the engine room of capitalism, dwelling

---

25   Heinz Bude, 'Das Legitimationsdefizit des "Keystroke-Kapitalismus"', epilogue to Sahr, *Das Versprechen des Geldes*, 389-392.

instead on capitalist economic practices and advocating their mitigation with wealth redistribution schemes. A more effective taxation of capital assets and legacies is surely indispensable if we are to counter the growing concentration of wealth. Such policies are difficult to implement, however, given the necessary exceptions (such as inherited company assets) and the existence of tax havens; nor do they go far enough. If the social question of our age continues to be debated exclusively at the level of financial reforms and redistributive policies, the fuel that drives the capitalist engine – namely the unlimited credit supply – will be left untouched. The structures described here are not affected by reforms to financial market regulation, such as increased equity requirements or staff reinforcements for banking authorities. Not even the Tobin tax or indeed a capital levy would materially affect the practices of keystroke capitalism. Therefore, we should refrain for a moment from talking about redistributive policies such as taxes or cosmetic prestige projects such as Basel III (and IV) or the expansion of the European banking union, and turn our attention instead to the practice that is responsible in large measure for the growth of debt, the crises of the bubble economy and rising material inequality. In order to reframe the social question for our own times, we need to talk about who in a democratic society should decide how much new money is produced and who should receive it. It is vital that both strands of the reform debate be integrated into any discussion of the para-economic privilege. The inequality crisis calls for a reform of the whole money creation system.

With this in mind, we will conclude by raising two questions which might feature on the agenda of any consensus-building campaign with regard to keystroke capitalism and keystroke inequality: Should we, in view of the highlighted legitimacy deficit, economize banks and democratize the keystrokes?

Should Banks Be Economized?

A variety of approaches to the re-economization of keystroke capitalism are currently in discussion under the heading of sovereign money reform, 100 percent money or positive money. Despite many differences in the details, these proposals – which, for simplicity's sake, I shall hereafter refer to collectively as *sovereign money reform* – all seek to abolish private money creation through credit. Discussion of these reforms is not confined to fringe groups and readerships: In the UK, the Positive Money Movement has evolved into a respected NGO with renowned economists among its ranks. As for the German-speaking countries, the Swiss sovereign money movement even managed to secure a referendum on reforming the money system. Political institutions, too, are already looking at these ideas, with the European Central Bank recently delivering its (unfavourable) verdict on the reforms.[26] The aim of the sovereign money movement is to abolish the banks' ability to produce purchasing power. The new money is labelled 'sovereign' and 'positive' because it would be debt-free – that is, purchasing power that is not generated by the act of borrowing and hence tied to a promise of repayment, as is the case today (we will consider where new money would come from instead in a moment). In a sovereign money system, anyone wanting to borrow from a bank would have to be given access to actual deposits, consisting of real assets and not just claims. If private banks were obliged in

---

26 For relevant accounts of the reform agenda, see Huber, *Monetäre Modernisierung*; Jackson and Dyson, *Modernising Money*. A report that attracted much attention, though it did not constitute an 'official' statement from the International Monetary Fund, was Jaromir Benes and Michael Kumhof, 'The Chicago Plan Revisited', *IMF Working Paper* 12/202, 2012. The German Bundesbank commented on plans of this kind in German Bundesbank, *Monthly Report April 2017*. Extensive references can be found at positivemoney.org, monetative.de and vollgeld-initiative.ch (the latter including details of the Swiss referendum).

this way to grant only pre-financed loans instead of money-generating credit, their para-economic VIP status would become a thing of the past. As such, their investment decisions would be based on ownership (savings) and they would (once again) become the capital logisticians that the economic mainstream still believes them to be. In seeking to restore the dependency of investments on ownership, sovereign money reformers thus envisage an *economization* of the (private) credit system.

Although the economization of capitalism may appear attractive in view of the findings of this book, there is at least one stumbling block to consider: the role that non–asset-based lending plays in societal dynamics. To make a trite yet important observation, economic practices rely on a constant supply of debt. Debt is not the result of miscalculations or wrong decisions, but an important and normal part of the production and reproduction process of goods and services. Borrowed capital is needed to fund new start-ups, adapt existing companies to changing conditions and overcome short-term liquidity problems of otherwise solid businesses. In a society with no facility for lending funds relatively quickly and flexibly, every cash shortage would result in bankruptcy – and that would be disastrous. So it is not surprising that a genuinely debt-free economy has probably never been attempted, and no coincidence that the earliest relics of major human settlements in Bronze Age Mesopotamia are IOUs.[27] Talk of reforming the money and debt system only makes sense on the assumption that, by their practices, economic actors generate and reproduce a permanent demand for borrowing options. Sovereign money reform does not seek to abolish debt, but to break the association of purchasing power with debt. In a sovereign money system, there would be no more credit but only *loans*,

---

27 William N. Goetzmann, *Money Changes Everything: How Finance Made Civilization Possible*, Princeton, 2016.

Should Banks Be Economized?

meaning that debts would serve to distribute existing purchasing power. The demand for borrowed purchasing power would have to be financed from the existing supply. Specifically, the borrowing requirements of economic actors in a sovereign money system would have to be funded by private-sector deficits – that is, by capital owners making their assets available to banks as loan resources. The owners would have to temporarily surrender their liquid funds: in other words, actually *save*. Unlike today, credit holders would have to be motivated to lend their purchasing power. And the only ones likely to be willing and able to do this would be those with more than they need to cover their short-term expenditures. This resource, limited to surplus funds, would be a stark contrast to the current hyperelastic credit supply; interest on borrowed assets would probably rise dramatically and end up back in the pockets of those capital owners who are in a position to lend. Loan financing would be dependent, at least indirectly, on the asset holders' consent, assuming that they would only deposit their savings (and hence make them available for loans) with a bank that would invest them at least broadly in line with their interests. As such, sovereign money reform, in its efforts to replace the dominance of capital producers with capital owners, would mean both an economic gain and a power gain for the wealthy. To say the least, such a restoration of *economic* capitalism is, as Ann Pettifor points out, not a 'progressive' project.[28]

Warnings can also come from another direction, however: The Austrian economic theorist Joseph Schumpeter, for instance, would probably have declared a system in which investments could only be financed by existing wealth to be doomed to paralysis.[29] If societies make the funding of their investments

---

28 Pettifor, *The Production of Money*, 112.
29 Joseph A. Schumpeter, *The Theory of Economic Development: An Inquiry into Profits, Capital, Credit, Interest and the Business Cycle*, Cambridge, MA, 1934, chapter 3. Schumpeter argues that the banker,

and innovations directly dependent on the consent of capital owners, they may end up stifling economic momentum and progress. Or so Schumpeter believed, and for a simple and profoundly sociological reason: Innovations depend on new combinations of existing resources, achieved by modifying established production processes and original or forgotten techniques, designs and materials. The trouble is that the capital owners needed to fund these new combinations (in a world of loans, without money-generating credit) have acquired their wealth using conventional combinations. Consequently, they are (with some exceptions) more sceptical of innovations than those economic forces that Schumpeter calls entrepreneurs, and who generate economic momentum with new combinations of existing resources.

Interestingly, we find a very similar picture today in the neoclassical mainstream of economic theory: here, savers are regarded as risk-averse actors, and borrowers as bold entrepreneurs willing to take a chance on new combinations. This heroic liberal narrative of innovative, good-guy businessmen and cautious savers should not be swallowed whole. For one thing – as we have seen – the lion's share of purchasing power generated by keystroke capitalism is not intended to create new combinations, but to inflate the value of existing assets. Indeed, investment in start-ups and new combinations has suffered due to this situation for years.[30] On the other hand, credit that generates purchasing power independently of available capital does have a potential for economic momentum that loans do not. This is particularly clear from historical studies examining the importance of the high and late medieval invention of value creation by chalking up debts (see

---

as a producer of purchasing power, 'stands between those who wish to form new combinations and the possessors of productive means'. Ibid., 74.

30 Rana Foroohar, *Makers and Takers: The Rise of Finance and the Fall of American Business*, New York, 2016.

Chapter Three) or the emergence of a money-issuing banking system to accommodate the explosion of economic growth in nineteenth-century Europe.[31] Without the possibility of flexible money creation via pen and paper (bank notes, bills and book money), the huge acceleration of economic growth that provided the material basis for many advances of the modern age would not have been possible, as experts widely agree. Credit – a currency created from nothing – shapes societies. If a society incorporates actors with the ability to create additional purchasing power by accepting a promise of repayment, then its scope for economic activity is, in a sense, unlimited. If it rejects this possibility because it considers debt-free money more rational, then the volume of fundable projects will be limited by the available supply. That is, until a political authority (as we shall see in a moment) decides to increase production. And, even then, the new purchasing power would first have to be absorbed by individuals or companies and solidified into private wealth before it can be deposited at a bank in the form of savings. Bridge financing to cover short-term cash shortfalls of otherwise solvent businesses and start-ups would be dependent on individual decisions to make money available for loans. The price of re-economizing capitalism – that is, of abolishing the creation of purchasing power based on a promise of repayment, would be a less liquid, less flexible and, at worst, less dynamic system.[32] Advocates of sovereign money reform rightly object here that a reduction of the available loan

---

[31] Geoffrey Ingham, *Capitalism*, Cambridge, 2008; Geoffrey M. Hodgson, *Conceptualizing Capitalism: Institutions, Evolution, Future*, Chicago, 2015; Jens Beckert, *Imagined Futures, Fictional Expectations and Capitalist Dynamics*, Cambridge, MA, 2016.

[32] For this critique, see Guiseppe Fontana and Malcom Sawyer, 'Full Reserve Banking: More "Cranks" Than "Brave Heretics"', *Cambridge Journal of Economics* 40(5), 2016, 1333–50; Yeva Nersisyan and L. Randall Wray, 'Modern Money Theory and the Facts of Experience', *Cambridge Journal of Economics* 40(5), 2016, 1297–316; Pettifor, *The Production of Money*.

capital would in fact be a jolly good thing if the overriding purpose is to avoid fuelling speculative bubbles. At the same time, they dismiss the fear that sovereign money systems could lead to a shortage of loans by arguing that the economization of banks would have to be complemented by a restoration of the political money creation privilege.

Should Money Creation Be Democratized?

The second key question we need to answer in view of the instabilities and inequities of keystroke capitalism concerns a familiar theme: To what extent can and should political actors be granted money creation privileges? Even a sovereign money system needs a money creation mechanism in order to allow the supply to be adapted to changing conditions (however they are defined). According to the reformers' vision, the money creation privilege would be split up and shared between two authorities: First, an expert committee of the central bank would decide, based on observed and predicted economic trends, how much extra purchasing power the economy needs. As for how that power then enters the economic cycle, various possibilities have been suggested. The initiative associated with the economist Joseph Huber favours a system whereby 'newly created money in the form of original seigniorage is brought into circulation via public spending'.[33] In other words, it would fall to the parliamentary budget planners to spend whatever amount the money creation committee generated. That way, new purchasing power would not be automatically created when and wherever a bank sensed a profitable business opportunity, but would enter the economy via public spending – on civil servant salaries, social security contributions (possibly a citizen's dividend), infrastructure projects or defence. Only once it had been absorbed in this manner could

---

33 Huber, 'Monetäre Modernisierung', 300.

it be fixed as savings deposits and lent by banks in the form of loans. As such, this reform promises a drastic reduction of the banks' room to manoeuvre, and an expansion of that of the state, which would be (re)gaining a whole new source of funding. If it were to be introduced, public spending could be financed either by borrowing or taxation or, alternatively, by fresh money. Thus, democratically sanctioned governments would be able to ensure that new money was not used *in the first instance* for the purchase of private assets, but for self-defined productive purposes (thereby breaking the asset price spiral).

What the practical consequences of greater political influence would be is open to question, however. In the scenario envisaged by the reformers, the central bank committee would be able to decide how much money to create without any input from government. Ideally, it would be as independent from parliament and government as the legal system. Indeed, the committee is sometimes alluded to as if it were a kind of constitutional authority: an independent 'monetary' branch alongside the legislative, executive and judiciary. Its remit, however, say the sovereign money theorists, would be restricted to two functions which would guide committee decisions, and against which they would be judged. One would be to prevent inflation, and the other to adapt the money supply to the 'overall economic growth potential'.[34] Consequently, the committee's scope for generating economic growth would be relatively small, as it would have to justify decisions about money production capacities on the basis of growth forecasts. At a time when capitalist economies appear to be afflicted by 'secular stagnation' and persistently low growth rates are anticipated across the board,[35] a monetary branch would channel precious

---

34 Huber, 'Monetäre Modernisierung', 304.
35 See Thomas Piketty, *Capital in the Twenty-First Century*, trans. Arthur Goldhammer, Cambridge, MA, 2014.

little new money into state coffers. The promised expansion of political influence could turn out to be an illusion. Besides, economic forecasts are not hard science, but contingent upon 'imagined futures'. This term was recently used by Jens Beckert, who reminds us of the importance of expectations about the future – in other words, the sociopolitical inspiration of a widespread trust in future prosperity – for the creation of economic momentum and rising wealth in a capitalist society.[36] Even if a monetary branch were to be established, there would still be no social arena where the future, and with it the necessary new purchasing power, could be democratically debated. In order to stimulate economic growth in phases of stagnation or regression – that is, when the imagined futures look bleak (and tax revenues fall accordingly) – governments would have to rely on loan capital from investors, as the committee would not be in a position to make fresh capital available.

But would that really be desirable? Earlier, we described money as constituting the ultimate capacity to get things done. Should the available supply of such a capacity really be made to depend on the calculations of a small committee of experts? In a system of this kind, society would have no more power to decide on its economic output than it does now. The monetary branch would replace the privatization of money creation with a depoliticized expertocracy. As Ann Pettifor notes, this would make life-or-death questions – such as whether society can afford the necessary measures to combat climate change – dependent upon the calculations of a single authority rather than on a public debate.[37]

Sovereign money reform is technocratic, undemocratic and potentially regressive. It is therefore unsurprising that the mooted alternatives (both to privatized money creation and sovereign money reform) should include, not least, a return to

---

36 Beckert, *Imagined Futures*.
37 Pettifor, *The Production of Money*.

the option of so-called monetary financing of public spending. Under this system, the state would fund its spending through credit that it produces itself – that is, via its own keystrokes. If governments can create money through their own spending, they can react flexibly to cyclical fluctuations and money shortages. That way, investments would no longer be subject to the whims of expert committees or the approval of capital owners. Socially, politically and ecologically inspired projects with low (or only very long-term) returns would no longer be in competition with other, more lucrative projects, such as real estate purchases, which are currently financed by banks at the touch of a button. Governments could (if they wished) cover the borrowing requirements of the real economy without regard either to the profit expectations of capital investors or to the growth forecasts of experts. Greater scope for state action would be guaranteed. This notion of state intervention in the money 'printing machines' is a red rag to many economic commentators. According to economic historian Werner Plumpe, for example, the liberation of central banks as money-creating institutions from the influence of political overlords represented a step forward for civilization in that it helped to 'combat overweening state power. With the invention and spread of paper money, the state's ability to create money suddenly became open to boundless exploitation via politically dependent central banks (the money-printing press).'[38] If the money creation privilege is invested in the state, it is feared, there is a strong pressure on politicians with governmental responsibility – particularly in democracies – to issue more and more funds in order to curry favour with the electorate. This state of affairs, it is argued, would have disastrous long-term consequences for economic development and social cohesion. According to the sovereign money reformers

---

38 Werner Plumpe, 'Bleibt also nur noch die Revolte?', *Frankfurter Allgemeine Zeitung*, 3 November 2015.

Andrew Jackson and Ben Dyson, therefore, 'neither profit-seeking bankers nor vote-seeking politicians can be trusted with the power to create money'.[39] Though relatable, this familiar expression of mistrust vis-à-vis democratically elected governments, on the basis that they are dependent on the whims of the masses and incapable of handling the money creation privilege, has grown somewhat stale. According to Adair Turner, the privatization of the money creation privilege in order to 'cure' the 'disease' of state-controlled money creation was 'as harmful as the disease' itself.[40] The private sector, it turns out, is no less profligate, as demonstrated by the growth of credit, the financialization process it has fuelled, and the inequality that has arisen as a result. Why, then, should a democratic government deprive itself of a powerful resource by placing it at the disposal of private actors who will only use it to create inequality and instability? If it comes to a choice between two allegedly irresponsible holders of the money creation privilege, one could argue that the lesser evil would be to plump for the one that is, at least in theory, democratically accountable: the government. If we cannot 'trust' the private sector (in Jackson and Dyson's sense of the word) to pursue a constructive and socially acceptable monetary policy, then it seems reasonable to trust a body that can be controlled and sanctioned by elections.

Admittedly, returning the money creation privilege to the political system has its own risks that should not be downplayed. The primary risk, as already discussed, is the possibility of excessive use, although that goes for *whoever* holds this privilege, not just governments. If we did have a democratic system of money creation, however – one that, instead of encouraging asset purchasing among private households, concentrated on stimulating real economic production and

---

39 Jackson and Dyson, *Modernising Money*, 204.
40 Turner, *Between Debt and the Devil*, 141.

consumption – it would likely replace asset price inflation with consumer price inflation. In that case, governments would be compelled to reduce the money supply through taxation. Taxes would have to be understood as an instrument of monetary policy and would thus probably lose some of their (already problematic) legitimacy.[41] If prices rose, states would be forced to reduce their own spending and if necessary raise taxes, and the 'pressure' to justify to the electorate what are likely to be pretty unpopular measures could not be minimized by blaming practical constraints or independent central banks (after all, holding all the power also means bearing all the responsibility). What's more, the burden of these monetary policy measures could not be spread evenly due to the existence of tax havens where large fortunes can be stashed away. In short, we would be wise to approach the proposal of keystroke democratization (entrusting the money creation privilege to governments) with the same prudence as that of the economization of banks (abolishing private money creation). It is of course possible to envisage additional measures allowing a mix of private and public money creation subject to suitable restrictions.[42] Regardless of whether we regard the idea of money-printing states as emancipatory or far too dangerous (or too much of a threat to our own privileges), however, the 'taboo' subject of monetary financing of the public sector is already back on the agenda when it comes to debating the future political structure of capitalism.[43]

---

41 If governments financed their spending via a deficit similar to the overdraft facility of private accounts, payments flowing back to the state (taxes and charges) would retrospectively reduce this deficit and the collected money would be cancelled out by the deficit reduction, just like paying back a bank loan today. For a detailed account of the cycles of political money production, see L. Randall Wray, *Modern Money Theory: A Primer on Macroeconomics for Sovereign Money Systems*, New York, 2012.
42 See Pettifor's proposal in *The Production of Money*.
43 Turner, *Between Debt and the Devil*.

#keystrokes

This book can only give a taste of the theoretical, economic, social and political challenges associated with the rise of keystroke capitalism, and of suggestions for change. Nevertheless, the crux of the argument is hopefully clear: The dynamic of financialization and its amplification of the inequality crisis cannot be understood without taking into account the money creation privilege. Accordingly, the dynamic interplay of economics and inequality can no longer be explained exclusively in terms of the dualism between the decisions of capital owners and the interventions of the sovereign state, as classical capitalist theories suggest, but must also be related to the decisions of para-economic capital producers. Their decisions to approve more and more debt while purchasing and producing more and more financial assets, shored up by comprehensive political support, have continually pushed up asset prices and returns from capital investments. These steadily rising returns allowed high earners to decouple their salaries from those of the rest of the workforce. At the same time, they also enticed more and more non-financial companies into the financial markets, thereby depressing the incomes of the wage-earning majority. In the search for alternative means of financing the prosperity promised by capitalism, the consumer credit market, boosted by deregulation, securitization and zero marginal cost production, offered a ready solution. The pressure on the average wages of the 'poorer 90 percent' and the lack of growth due to the outflow of investment capital from the real economy to the financial one undermined the chances of large swathes of the population to participate in the expansion of the financial sector and the benefits of unrestrained money creation. As a result, the wealth-boosting effects of credit – what I call 'keystroke returns' – became concentrated at the top of the global wealth pyramid. This inequality, then, is due in no small part to a simple keystroke. Given the increasing concentration of income and wealth at the top, the alarmingly high debt mountain, the striking frequency of financial crises and a sluggish, investment-starved real economy, it is, at the very least, no longer enough to go on discussing the measures proposed so far. Private and political resources are needed to tackle the problems of the present and the challenges of the future. The status quo might be the most dangerous option. The much invoked 'crisis of democracy'[44] may also be symptomatic of a fatalistic mood in which the prospects of economic stagnation instead of growth and (in many regions) high unemployment have destroyed any hope of effectively combating economic inequality. Redistribution and regulation policies seem powerless in the face of a globalized and financialized system, having all but lost their grip on the refuges of wealthy elites and volatile capital flows. At the same time, public authorities everywhere plead scarcity of funds amid austerity policies that are currently afflicting whole generations of unemployed young people in southern Europe, as well as the UK's National Health Service, asylum seekers and the left-behind in Germany and elsewhere.

The project to democratize keystroke capitalism offers a way out of these constraints and the fatalism they foster. In reserve currency blocs at least, and given sufficient political will, the para-economy could be brought under democratic control by the respective home countries. Whatever decision individual readers – and indeed all of us as a political collective – may reach on this matter, anyone who is serious about managing financialization and combating the inequality crisis must consider the democratization of keystroke capitalism, and perhaps even give it a try. Despite all the understandable doubts regarding alternatives to the privatized para-economic privilege, the onus is ultimately on the sceptics to acknowledge the economic and social failure of

---

44 Rosanvallon, *The Society of Equals*.

an experiment in which the private sector enjoys the exclusive right to produce money from nothing. And it is the sceptics' responsibility to open themselves up to the possibility of alternatives.

Index

Abolafia, Mitchel, 61
Adam, Klaus, 82
Ahearne, Alan, 18
Allen, Franklin, 61
Alvaredo, Facundo, 1, 3
Alvarez, Ignacio, 17
Ancient Greece, 91
Apple, 84
Aristotle, 44, 91
Arnoldi, Jakob, 25
Atkinson, Anthony B., 2, 7, 30
August, Friedrich, 107
Aveling, Edward, 47
Ayadi, Rym, 86

Baecker, Dirk, 43, 44
Balhorn, Loren, 47, 100
Bank of England, 13, 24, 61, 83
Bank, Julian, 105
Barba, Aldo, 19
Basel III, 112
Battiston, Stefano, 88
Baxendale, Toby, 9
Beckert, Jens, 39, 44, 61, 117, 120

Benediktsdottir, Sigridur, 87
Benes, Jaromir, 113
Benmelech, Efraim, 28
Bezemer, Dirk, 81, 95
Bhattacharya, Sudipto, 61
Black-Scholes model, 27
Blommestein, Hans, 15
Boltanski, Luc, 47
Bourguignon, François, 2
Brandes, Sören, 42
Brandmeir, Kathrin, 5, 12, 19
Brecht, Bertolt, 90
Brennan, Simon, 13, 90
Bretton Woods, 20, 59, 90
Bude, Heinz, 7, 88, 102, 111
Burawoy, Michael, 102

Camiller, Patrick, 2, 18, 74, 100
Canada, 15, 29
Cassidy, John, 61
Cecchetti, Stephen, 18
Centeno, Miguel, 39
Cetorelli, Nicola, 85, 86
Chancel, Lucas, 1

Index

Chavagneux, Christian, 23
Chiapello, Eve, 47
China, 1
Cohen, Jeffrey C., 108
Cohen, Joseph, 39
Cook, Tim, 84
Cremers, K. J. Martijn, 85
Croce, R. Della, 15
Crotty, James, 85
Crouch, Colin, 2, 34

Damocles, 71
Danielsson, Jon, 87
Darcillon, Thibault, 33
Daruvala, Toos, 2, 12
Davies, James, 1, 5
Davis, Gerald F., 11, 61
Debelle, Guy, 18
Deutsche Bundesbank, 64, 65
Dillard, Dudley, 44
DiPrete, Thomas A., 31
Dlugosz, Jennifer, 28
Dobbs, Richard, 2, 12
Dörre, Klaus, 47
Dünhaupt, Petra, 31
Dyson, Ben, 81, 109, 121, 122

Edison, Thomas, 16
Eirich, Gregory M., 31
Elder-Vass, Dave, 8, 40
Elliott, Gregory, 47
Engels, Frederick, 49

Esposito, Elena, 27
European Central Bank, 81, 83, 84, 113

Fagan, Teresa Lavender, 23
Fama, Eugene, 61, 66
Fernbach, David, 2, 18, 74, 100
Financial Market Promotion Acts, 23
Fligstein, Neil, 34
Fontana, Guiseppe, 117
Foroohar, Rana, 80, 116
Förster, Michael, 3
France, 1, 3, 17, 29
Frey, Bruno S., 95
Friedman, Milton, 4, 107, 108
Froud, Julie, 32
Fulcher, James, 47

Galbraith, James K., 2, 82
Gale, Douglas, 61
GE Capital, 16
General Electric, 16
General Motors, 16, 33
German Bundesbank, 113
Germany, 15, 21, 23, 29, 81, 100, 105, 125
Gilomen, Hans-Jörg, 56
Gindin, Sam, 15, 40, 86
Glattfelder, James B., 88
Glick, Reuven, 18
God, 91

Index

Goda, Thomas, 6, 15, 82
Goetzmann, William N., 25, 55, 114
Goldberg, Linda, 85
Goldhammer, Arthur, 2, 4, 29, 76, 100, 119
Goldstein, Adam, 34
Graeber, David, 44, 55
Greenham, Tony, 63, 109
Grimm, Michaela, 5, 12

Haldane, Andrew, 13, 80, 90
Hale, Travis, 82
Haslam, Colin, 32
Hayek, Friedrich, 107
Helfrich, Silke, 8
Herrmann, Jan-Peter, 47
Herstatt, 24
Hillebrandt, Frank, 44
Hirte, Katrin, 62
Hodgson, Geoffrey M., 39, 117
Hodgson, Graham, 95
Höffe, Otfried, 108
Holzhausen, Arne, 5, 12
Honegger, Claudia, 27
Howe, Sharon, iii, 66
Huang, Rocco, 85
Huber, Joseph, 64, 80, 93, 109, 118
Hudson, Michael, 81
Huisman, Wim, 87
Hunt, Emery Kay, 48
Hviding, Ketil, 20

Iceland, 86, 87
Ingham, Geoffrey, 39, 46, 57, 75, 77, 104, 117
International Monetary Fund (IMF) 24, 110
Iversen, Torben, 75

Jackson, Andrew, 81, 109, 121, 122
Jakab, Zoltan, 61
Johal, Sukhdev, 32

Keen, Steve, 2, 92
Kersting, Wolfgang, 107
Kieserling, André, 109
Kim, Jerry W., 31
Kim, Suntae, 11, 61
Klein, Hans-Joachim, 61
Klein, Michael A., 61
Kocka, Jürgen, 75
Kogut, Bruce, 31
Kopp, Johannes, 45, 61
Kraemer, Klaus, 64, 80, 109
Krippner, Greta, 11, 13
Kristal, Tali, 29
Krugman, Paul, 61
Kumhof, Michael, 6, 61, 113
Kuznets, Simon, 2

La Porta, Rafael, 87
Laeven, Luc, 110
Lansing, Kevin J., 18
Lastra, Rosa M., 86
Lautzenheiser, Mark, 48

Index

Lee, Benjamin, 25
Lessenich, Stephan, 47, 76
Lin, Ken-Hou, 14, 16
LiPuma, Edward, 25
Llena-Nozal, Ana, 3
Lluberas, Rodrigo, 1, 5
Locke, John, 107
López-de-Silanes, Florencio, 87
Lucarelli, Bill, 22
Luhmann, Niklas, 43, 45, 46, 55, 101
Lund, Susan, 2, 12
Lütz, Susanne, 12, 20, 61
Lysandrou, Photis, 6, 15, 82

MacKenzie, Donald, 27
MacLaren, Michelle, 37
Madouros, Vasileios, 13, 90
Magnin, Chantal, 27
Mahar, Molly, 20
Mandel, Benjamin H., 28
Marks, Stephen G., 39
Martino, Antonio, 46
Marx, Karl, 40, 47–49
Mason, J. W., 85
Mason, Paul, 8
Mau, Steffen, 7, 75, 95, 103
Maurer, Andrea, 12, 44, 61
McAndrews, James, 86
Mellor, Mary, 63, 109
Merkel, Wolfgang, 75
Mertens, Daniel, 18
Michael North, Michael, 58
Mikl-Horke, Gertraude, 44

Milan Zafirovski, Miguel, 44, 61
Milanovic, Branko, 2, 7, 30
Millo, Yuval, 27
Mishkin, Frederic S., 61
Mizruchi, Mark, 61
Mohanty, M. S., 18
Mokyr, Joel, 58
Moore, Basil J., 66
Moore, Samuel, 47
Morgan, Donald, 28
Murphy, Richard, 23

Nachtwey, Oliver, 100
Nafilyan, Vahé, 3
Neal, Larry, 25
Neckel, Sighard, 27, 32, 105
Nee, Victor, 39
Nersisyan, Yeva, 117
Nessel, Sebastian, 64, 80, 109
Nesvetailova, Anastasia, 23
Nixon, Richard, 43
Nordhaus, William, 91
Noss, Joseph, 24
Nozick, Robert, 107, 108

Olivares-Caminal, Rodrigo, 86
Orléan, André, 43
Ötsch, Walter, 62

Pahl, Hanno, 62
Palan, Ronen, 23
Panitch, Leo, 15, 40, 86

Index

Pettifor, Ann, 2, 63, 92, 100, 115, 120
Philippon, Thomas, 12
Piketty, Thomas, 1, 2, 29, 76, 119
Pinkman, Jesse, 72, 96
Pittinsky, Matthew, 31
Pivetti, Massimo, 19
Plumpe, Werner, 121
Postberg, Christian, 57
Pühringer, Stephan, 62

Rancière, Romain, 6
Redner, Joachim, 27
Reifner, Udo, 53
Reinhart, Carmen, 110
Reshef, Ariell, 12
Rifkin, Jeremy, 8, 90
Rognlie, Matthew, 81
Rogoff, Kenneth, 110
Rosa, Hartmut, 47
Rosanvallon, Pierre, 4, 76, 100
Ryan-Collins, Josh, 63, 109

Sahr, Aaron, iii, 10, 43, 60, 88, 92, 109
Samuelson, Paul, 91
Sautner, Zacharias, 85
Savage, Robert, 27
Sawyer, Malcom, 117
Schäfers, Bernhard, 45, 61
Schäuble, Wolfgang, 61, 66
Schenk, Catherine, 21

Schöneck, Nadine M., 7, 75, 95, 103
Schularick, Moritz, 93
Schumpeter, Joseph, 42, 43, 85, 115, 116
Schuster, Peter, 57
Scott-Railton, Thomas, 2
Shorrocks, Anthony, 1, 5, 133, 134
Signori, Gabriela, 57
Singh, Manmohan, 82
Smelser, Neil, 61
Smith, Adam, 4, 44
Soener, Matthew, 16
Sowerbutts, Rhiannon, 24
Sparsam, Jan, 44
Staab, Philipp, 7, 88
Stearns, Linda, 61
Stella, Peter, 82
Stiglitz, Joseph, 7
Streeck, Wolfgang, 2, 18, 49, 74–76, 100
Swanson, Paul, 39
Swedberg, Richard, 39, 61

Taylor, Alan, 93
Thakor, Anjan V., 61
Tobin tax, 112
Tomaskovic-Devey, Donald, 14, 16, 17, 22, 23
Traina, James, 86
Turner, Adair, 13, 79, 80, 90, 109, 122
Tzamourani, Panagiota, 82

Index

Unger, Robert, 67

Valencia, Fabián, 110
Vitali, Stefania, 88
Vogl, Joseph, 27

Wagner, Gert G., 103, 106
Weatherall, James Owen, 27
Wei, Chenyang, 28
Weingast, Barry R., 75
Wells, Robin, 61
Welskopp, Thomas, 40, 42
Werner, Richard, 61, 63, 65, 109
White, Walter, 71, 72, 74, 96
Will, Susan, 87
Williamson, John, 20
Windolf, Paul, 32

Winston, Kenneth, 46
Winterkorn, Martin, 105
Wittman, Donald A., 75
Wolff, Guntram B., 18
Woolley, Paul, 13, 80, 90
Wray, L. Randall, 9, 63, 67, 92, 117, 123

Xenophon, 44

Yang, Jae-Suk, 31
Young, Brigitte, 34

Zamarripa, Guillermo, 87
Zampolli, Fabrizio, 18
Zierenberg, Malte, 42
Zoega, Gylfi, 87
Zucman, Gabriel, 23